The PATH TO SURRENDER

Finding your way back to the flock

Julie Anne Fehrenbacher

The Path to Surrender
ISBN 978-0-578-98665-4
Published by 3 Lemmings Press
Facebook.com/ThePathtoSurrender

© 2021 Julie Anne Fehrenbacher. All rights reserved.
This book or any portion thereof may not be reproduced or used in any manner whatsoever without the express written permission of the publisher except for the use of brief quotations in a book review or scholarly journal.

Unless otherwise noted, Scripture quotations are taken from THE HOLY BIBLE, NEW INTERNATIONAL VERSION®, NIV® Copyright © 1973, 1978, 1984, 2011 by Biblica, Inc.® Used by permission. All rights reserved worldwide.

Scripture quotations marked ESV® Bible (The Holy Bible, English Standard Version®), Copyright © 2001 by Crossway, a publishing ministry of Good News Publishers. Used by permission. All rights reserved.

Scripture quotations marked NLT are taken from the Holy Bible, New Living Translation, copyright © 1996, 2004, 2015 by Tyndale House Foundation. Used by permission of Tyndale House Publishers, Inc., Carol Stream, Illinois 60188. All rights reserved.

Scripture quotations marked TPT are taken from The Passion Translation®. Copyright © 2017 BroadStreet Publishing ® Group, LLC. Used by permission. All rights reserved.

Edited by Dana L. Cobb
Design by Monica Thomas for TLC Book Design,
TLCBookDesign.com

Imagery from Adobe Stock.
Cover: *Coming Home* illustration © grandfailure, sheep © Viktoria.
Interior: Butterfly lifecycle © Marina Gorskaya, butterfly ©jenesesimre, branch © jeystyle, butterfly cluster © Gluiki, flowers ©val_iva

Printed in the United States of America

Dedication

I dedicate this book to everyone I have encountered in my life so far, whether we were connected for a reason, a season, or a lifetime. Whether our connection was pleasant or unpleasant or indifferent, you have been significant on my "path to surrender," a light along the way. I am thankful to you all! Each of you was a piece of the "God thread" that wrapped around me and has now become my wings to fly freely in surrender to God's will for my life.

I offer a special dedication to Rose. Now at home with her Heavenly Father, but on Earth, a Christian mentor who set an example for me of what it looks like to be a disciple. I was on the outskirts of the flock and she pulled me in. Thank you, Rose!

To the women God sent to light my path:

- Kathleen: you re-ignited my fire
- Julie: the grace-giver
- Sandy: you offered me hope
- Jami: my prayer warrior

To my mom, dad, and sister, that God may create new life in our family through this work.

Lastly, to my boys, Rylie and Sam, God breathed new life into me through you. I am so thankful He trusted me to care for you and guide you. You make my life so full and I experience God richly through our life together.

I love you.

To
Ruby Christine
&
Viola Philomena

may this heal generations.

Author's Note

I began writing this book eight years ago. At the time, I was married with a son who was about two years old. God's presence in my life had become very real and I felt Him whispering to me to write about the instructions He was giving me. Nudging me to share how I "hear Him" so that I may encourage others to listen and watch for His presence in their lives. The Spirit was moving me significantly to write these stories and glorify His name. The pressure of life mounted with working full time, a marriage in crisis, parenting, a second pregnancy, and eventually a divorce. I took a pause writing this; however, God's presence was peaking in my life. I was hearing Him loud and clear and more obediently and faithfully following His instructions. I stand today, calm, firm in my beliefs, and remain faithful. I made it to the other side of a mountain of obstacles. I was enslaved to many fears of the world, and through Jesus was able to shed the things that were enslaving me and freely run into his arms, surrendering and seeking His shelter. Our Father did as He promised in Psalm 40. He heard my cry, reached down and grabbed me out of the muck and the mire, put my feet on a rock, and gave me a firm place to stand. He put a new song in my mouth, a hymn of praise to our God. My hope is that this book is my chance to share a hymn of praise to our God with you so that you may embrace His presence in your life and consider, begin, or continue your path to surrender.

Father, I humbly ask that the words in this book will provide only healing and no harm to Your people. I trust that the Spirit will move through the words to reach each reader in a way that speaks individually to him or her, leading them to a deeper truth, healing, and relationship with You. Thank You Father for this opportunity to connect with Your sons and daughters so we may know You better.

        My love to you all,
        Julie

CONTENTS

Prologue: I know what God is doing 3
Introduction 6

Part 1: Caterpillar — 11

Chapter 1 I See You 12
Chapter 2 "I Got This!" 23
Chapter 3 To My Knees 40

Part 2: Chrysalis — 51

Chapter 4 Finding Fellowship 52
Chapter 5 Rylie "And God breathed new life into me" .. 61
Chapter 6 Pressure is Mounting 79
Chapter 7 The Muck and the Mire 94
Chapter 8 Sam "And God taught me to let it go" 104

Part 3: Butterfly — 125

Chapter 9 Becoming a Butterfly 126

Epilogue 145
Resources 146
References 149
A Special Thank You 155
About the Author 156

Prologue
I know what God is doing…

As we grow in our faith, it can be a dangerous habit to think we are figuring out how God is working in our life. You catch yourself at times say, "I see what you are doing here." Then things work out completely different than you expected, sometimes better, sometimes worse, and you think, "Well I was off." You can almost hear God chuckle as He looks down and says, "Silly child, when will you stop trying to figure me out." It isn't that I want to know more than God or think I will ever fully understand Him, but that need for control always creeps back up.

> That need for control always creeps back up.

I am happy to say I have now embraced being a servant of the Lord. I hope when I enter into Heaven my Father is proud of the work I have done here on Earth. I hope I make Him smile, the way my children make me smile when I am so proud of the fine young men they are becoming. I am especially proud when they really show me that they have learned a valuable lesson and, more importantly, how to apply it to the next situation that comes up. I like to think our Father is the same way—tough on us, allowing us to stumble; however, so proud when we don't run away from our mistakes, but instead dust ourselves off and say, "I'll get it next time Father, you'll see!" Then, when we do get it, He and the angels are roaring in Heaven so proud of their little one on Earth.

But there are those times I get ahead of God's plan. Where I think I know just where He is headed with a plan and my mind goes there first and then I am disappointed when things aren't happening the way I expect or hope. Even more frustrating is when I know I am ready for something to happen, but it doesn't happen on my timeline. Sigh. Then I pick myself up and say, "Oh, this or that must happen first, then it will be the moment for this desire or need to occur." NOTHING Again. "Oh, He must have THIS in mind." NOT. "I give up, what are you doing Father?!" That final surrender is what He is waiting on, right? When we realize yet again we fell into the trap of thinking we are in control and have things figured out. After all the scenarios in our head don't happen, we are reminded how vulnerable we are, how much we really do need Him to lead our every step. He needs our complete trust, each day, even if the things that are happening don't make sense or seem in the order or timing we anticipated. It is called faith. We need faith in the big stuff and the small stuff, faith when it makes sense and faith when it doesn't, and faith when we are content and faith when we are not.

> *He needs our complete trust, each day, even if the things that are happening don't make sense.*

I picture this: sometimes, God is leading you along and then you feel like He dumped you in the middle of the ocean in a life raft with no oars. You see no land and have no way of moving. You are thinking, "Now what?" There is no way I can get out of this situation. No way in our humble human self can we escape alone. That is when we need Him most. No oar to get to shore, no direction to go, but God can surpass all human obstacles. He sends Jesus across those waves to our raft to grab our hand and walk with us across the water to just the right destination with all of the things we need. It is like we have to get to that place of complete surrender with no false thinking that "we've got this." We'll never "have it" without trusting that "He has it." We just have to *wait for His instructions* so that the best outcome, the necessary outcome, God's will, takes place. Amen!

I look forward to you joining me as I share about my surrender. I hope we can connect and find a place to meet wherever you are so that we may move further along the path to surrender together.

Introduction

Life Cycles

> *"For everything there is a season, A time for every activity under heaven. A time to be born and a time to die. A time to plant and a time to harvest...."* ~ECCLESIASTES 3:1-8 (NLT)

As you begin reading this book, you will notice a theme of two cycles

One cycle is referenced at the end of each chapter, shown below. It is a theme I found running through my surrender experiences that aligns with Spread Truth's *Story Maker.*[1] You will notice the area of the cycle highlighted in each chapter and the cycle repeats itself throughout the book. I encourage you to find the parallel in your own story to this story "cycle."

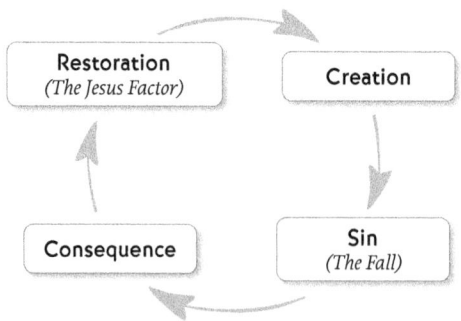

Without the Restoration (The Jesus Factor), we ping pong back and forth between sin and consequence. The cycle is incomplete until Jesus enters the picture to restore us to create new again.

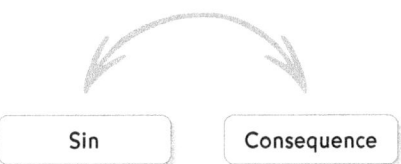

The second cycle refers to that of a caterpillar transforming into a butterfly. This book is divided into three sections. Chapters 1 through 3 fall in the caterpillar portion of surrender. Chapters 4 through 8 wrap you up in the chrysalis moment of surrender. The book concludes with Chapter 9 where you emerge in the butterfly stage of surrender.

I encourage you to see which stage of surrender you are in as you journey along with me!

Without restoration, we ping pong back and forth between sin and consequence.

Surrender

> *"Ask, and it will be given to you; seek, and you will find; knock, and it will be opened to you."* ~MATTHEW 7:7

When you hear the word surrender, what do you envision? Is it someone waving a white flag saying they give up? A dictionary may yield this definition, "to cease resistance to an enemy or opponent and submit to their authority.[1]" Surrender is a verb, an action step. It requires a choice.

The surrender I will be speaking about throughout this book is not one that asks you to stop resisting an enemy. In fact it is the opposite. It is to stop surrendering to "the enemy," and stop resisting God's authority. It is asking you to make a choice to give all authority for your life back to God, our creator, and stop resisting His will for our lives. He is so loving that He gives us choice, free will. He gives us freedom to choose Him; He does not force us.

> *"For the battle is not yours, but God's."* ~ 2 CHRONICLES 20:15

Surrender is difficult and occurs in many stages and layers. All at once it may seem overwhelming and seemingly impossible; however, with God, all things are possible!

At the end of each chapter, you will receive an opportunity to surrender various aspects of your life. I hope you will take a moment to pause. Take a deep breath and release it, and speak the statement out loud.

Then, wait.

Our God will answer. It may be immediate, it may not be. The answer may be through a phone call, email, or letter you've waited on or it may not look like what you anticipated at all. You may even get an answer that looks to be a new problem. The answer may be silence. Trust that the answer you receive is what you needed and let God's truth wash over you. Trust.

Then, keep asking, keep seeking, and keep knocking, and watch as God reveals Himself to you and becomes your friend and wise counselor.

Part 1
The Caterpillar

When we start this life, we are like a caterpillar: vulnerable creatures, crawling along looking to meet our needs for survival. A focus on self as we figure the world out. We are living in black and white only seeing what is immediately in front of us, like the leaf. We munch on quite a few leaves before we have fed ourselves enough of "earthly" things that we are ready to begin transforming to our higher self. We shed our skin several times as we are learning life lessons that are preparing us for the bigger transformation to occur.

Chapter 1
I See You

"Before I formed you in the womb I knew you, before you were born I set you apart." ~JEREMIAH 1:5

I see you.

I am proud of you.

I am amazed by you.

I want to spend more time with you.

You are a rare and wonderful creation of mine and
I smile at the thought of you.

I imagine our Father sitting in Heaven lovingly watching over you with these words right now. So thankful that you are choosing to be still and present to hear His voice and remember who He made you to be. *(Zephaniah 3:17; James 4:8)*

He has anticipated this moment.

The exact moment when you realize He is who He says He is. That He remains the only real truth you will find on this Earth that never changes. Despite all that has happened to you up until now, He has seen it, felt it.

He felt when you grieved the loss you experienced with no hope of relief. He felt when that individual hurt you so badly you doubted His existence. He caught every tear from your eye that fell in despair, and He wept with you. He smiled when you achieved all you had worked so hard for and thought, "That is the son and daughter I created!"

> *"It is the Lord who goes before you. He will be with you; he will not leave you or forsake you. Do not fear or be dismayed."*
> ~DEUTERONOMY 31:8 (ESV)

Your "ness" has been with you since birth. Actually, before that, since your Father breathed you into existence. What is "ness"? It is that something that makes you unique and special, a one of a kind. Not sure if you have seen *You, Me, and Dupree*[1], but it is a funny (slightly inappropriate movie) about a friend who moves in with his recently married buddy. The character of Owen Wilson talks about "ness" when his friend starts to lose who he is. He asks his friend where his "Carl-ness" has gone? I love that. That thing that makes us just who WE are and no one else is or can be. The God factor, our "X" factor, which no one can ever take from us.

> *"For God so loved the world that He gave his one and only Son...."*
> ~JOHN 3:16

Take a moment and consider: For God so loved the world that He gave His one and only _____ (insert your name).

Yes, He feels just as special about you and your existence because He sees us as His sons and daughters. The proud parent who designed the intricacies of our "ness" thought His world needed you! His world needed you with your "ness" to bring about the restoration Jesus was leading us to.

Wow! You are rare and wonderful.

I have dedicated a significant amount of time to ponder what my "ness" is. Seeking my purpose, gaining wisdom, and attempting to have a better understanding of God and His plan for us. After reading Rick Warren's *Purpose Driven Life*[2] for the third time (each time equally beneficial to my spiritual growth!), I finally took the prompting further to complete my own purpose statement which he encourages the reader to do. Here is what I developed:

> *My life purpose is to love the Lord with all my heart, soul, and mind while helping others find their "ness," that which makes them unique and special. I will utilize my spiritual gifts to help those the Lord puts on my path as the Spirit refines my fruits (Galatians 5:22-23) and helps me fulfill the Beatitudes (Matthew 5:1-12) on my road back to Him. Together, that I may assist Him by herding His sheep back to the flock.*
> (Developed Spring 2020)

One step further, I came across a Venn diagram provided by ProjectHappiness.org[3] which helped me to explore what I was put here to do.

Now, as I sit here writing this to you, the world may see me as: A divorced, single mom, who walked away from a great career to homeschool her children and dig deeper spiritually.

OR, we could look at it through God's lens and see that He did something amazing by: Delivering His daughter from an unhealthy union, set her feet on a rock, sheltered her and her children under His provision, and put a new song in her mouth to tell the world of His greatness.

I like that! One better, ponder this verse:

> *"You go before me and follow me. You place your hand of blessing on my head."* ~PSALM 139:5 (NLT)

Our Father went before you and prepared me, through my struggles, failings, imperfections, and deliverance, to write these words. He went so far as to send me to a Christian women's writing conference when I did not have the funds to do so. He led me to leave my children for the first time overnight to make that happen. He led me out of a marriage, out of a successful career, through the selling of my home, and through a pandemic. He walked me through a painful season of heartbreak, despair, and devastation. And then, the Lord offered me an opportunity. He placed me in my home, with my children. He filled me with peace, provided me time, and said, "It is time to write your brothers and sisters, my children, a love letter. I have gone before them and prepared you for this. Can you help me?"

It is time to write your brother and sisters a love letter.

I said yes.

You are rare and wonderful. So wonderful, that the pain I have experienced throughout my life melts away as I type these words in excitement of how God will use my pain to unite our stories with His and bring about continued restoration here on Earth!

The caterpillar

We all have a beginning to our story here on Earth. Most of us don't remember much until after we are three years old.[4] It is hard to believe that despite our understanding and memory of those first years, God knew us well. He knew us better than our parents, better than our siblings, better than the doctors and nurses who delivered us.

That beginning is our caterpillar stage. The time when our view of the world is very limited, like the leaf and immediate surroundings of a caterpillar. What we need is literally right in front of us. We seek and search for little. We are easily passed over, and victim to predators. Our protection during this stage is very important.

> God knows us better than our parents, our siblings, better than the doctors and nurses who delivered us.

Despite God's great plan for us and understanding of us, we begin this life seemingly unaware of Him. If you are a parent, you may have experienced that when your child whom you care for and have completely devoted your life to doesn't realize how much you do for them. Well, God gets it as most of His children do the same thing to Him and He doesn't even complain about it! He just waits patiently, loving us until we find our way back.

Blessed are those who end up in a family who begins talking about Jesus early, making His presence a mainstay in the home. A source of peace and joy to turn to in the good and the bad. However, not all of us begin our journey this way. Many of us are born into homes where our leaders have knowingly or unknowingly strayed from the flock (by flock, I mean our Heavenly Father's flock). Where the earthly matters like finances, possessions, worries, concerns, physical ailments, you name it, take the focus away from our Creator leading us away from His immediate care and into the valley of the shadow of death where evil lurks and the enemy preys over stray sheep. Ill-equipped to realize the seriousness of this straying, we find ourselves darting about to things which bring more immediate gratification like unhealthy relationships, food, substance abuse, gambling, excessive work, sleep, or a number of other conditions to fill the void in our life that can only be filled by being in the light of our Shepherd and under His rod and staff.

> *"Even though I walk through the valley of the shadow of death, I will fear no evil, for you are with me; your rod and your staff, they comfort me."* ~PSALM 23:4 (ESV)

Have you ever lost a pet or seen an animal get scared and start to run away? They run in a manner that is out of fear and often they get themselves into more trouble, running into the road, into the danger of a predator, or out into nature where they are lost from their safe home. Before long they have either been harmed, adapted to their new surroundings, or if fortunate, found their way back home.

We are no different; we run this way and that trying to seek out peace, love, and joy, continuing to fall short of really feeling those things. We wonder what we are doing wrong. I believe the majority of us are trying to be honest, care for one another, work hard, and be morally upright. It still isn't enough. We find ourselves missing something. Sometimes we just can't put our finger on it, so we keep seeking or give up and settle into circumstances that we shouldn't. This dangerous place of settling can entangle us behind a hedgerow of thorn bushes, separating us from the flock, and can take a mighty force to break through.

You will hear me reference "the flock" throughout this book. The flock refers to "our flock." That group of people our Father has put here on Earth to lead us home. "Our people." Those whom He has called to follow and obey Him and join together to create His church until He returns. By church, He isn't referencing a building:

> *"The church, you see, is not peripheral to the world; the world is peripheral to the church. The church is Christ's body, in which he speaks and acts, by which he fills everything with his presence."* ~EPHESIANS 1:23

If we aren't careful, we can be on the other side so long that the hedgerows have grown so thick we cannot see through them, and hope begins to fade. That gleam in our eye starts to dim and we wonder, "Is this all there is?" Some even begin to question if a Heavenly Father exists and if He is good.

After years of little to no acknowledgment of God, followed by settling into a life that is "working," and a hope in something better lost, away from the flock, the enemy has us right where he wants us. Alone and with no hope of something better or with an unbelief that better even exists. Who is that enemy? Satan, which in Hebrew means "adversary." Yep, he exists and works relentlessly to dim our "ness."

> *"Be alert and of sober mind. Your enemy the devil prowls around like a roaring lion looking for someone to devour."* ~1 PETER 5:8

Well my friends, we are all in this together. We are all sheep finding our way back, so let me take you on a journey along my own path to surrender. Where I found my way to our flock and back to our Shepherd. Where I am cared for, filled with love, joy, peace, and contentment. Where I have hope. I write these words today as I run along the countryside spreading this hope to you, God's sheep. I know you are longing for more, but unsure it exists. We will knock down those hedgerows of thorn bushes and run back to our Shepherd together in masses.

Will you join me on the path to surrender?

Today, I surrender:
my purpose.

*Lord, show me
the next step
I must take.*

Chapter 1
Goals & Discussion

What is your "ness"?

"Before I formed you in the womb I knew you, before you were born I set you apart." ~JEREMIAH 1:5

This part of the story sits in the "Creation" portion of our cycle. We began as a new creation breathed into existence by God. Let's celebrate our existence which was a day celebrated by our Father!

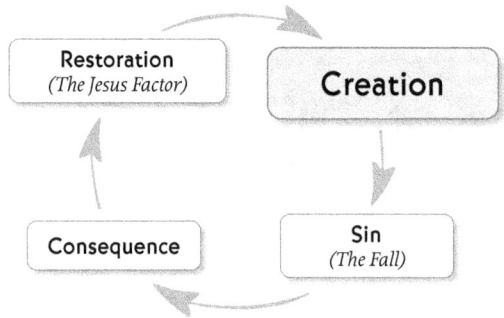

Action Step

Take time to explore your "ness." Celebrate the unique traits you were blessed with and contemplate God's great plan for your life.

1. What makes you unique and special? Complete this Venn diagram.

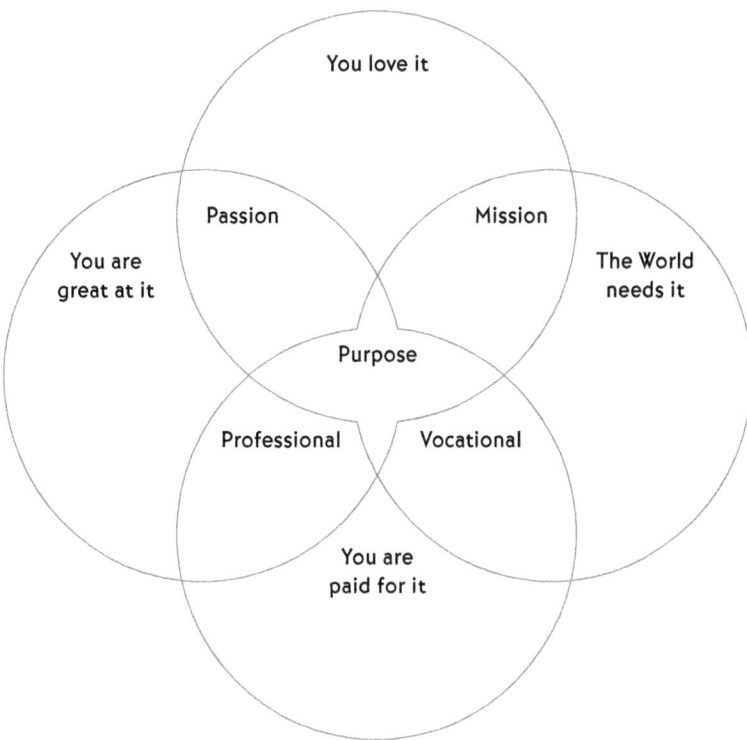

2. Write a purpose statement for your life: Rick Warren's *Purpose Driven Life*, Chapter 40 has great questions to prompt you if you need a start!

Spiritual Gifts analysis

3. 1 Corinthians 12 speaks about the Spiritual Gifts with which God has enabled us. Please read that chapter and begin to better understand yours! *Here is one example of an online assessment. You may find your own options, or if you are established in a church, ask if they have their own! https://gifts.churchgrowth.org/spiritual-gifts-survey/*

Chapter 2
"I Got This!"

"Do not be anxious about anything, but in every situation, by prayer and petition, with thanksgiving, present your requests to God. And the peace of God, which transcends all understanding, will guard your hearts and your minds in Christ Jesus."
~PHILIPPIANS 4:6-7

I wish I could say this Bible verse described me in my adolescent and young adult years, but it doesn't at all! I was a control person; anyone relate? Everything had its place, was on a list to be checked off, and was always organized. Things had to flow in an order that made sense to me. Almost an obsession over details. I remember my parents telling me I used to have an organizational system in my room as a child where I had bags everywhere and knew exactly which bags held which items. I was a good student, had an orderly room, locker, and later, dorm. However, inside I was a little bit of an anxious mess. I honestly hate to admit that. Which is another control thing! I wanted to be relaxed and go with the flow, but that was a struggle for me.

Being in control has its perks. Usually you excel at earthly matters like deadlines, whether academic or professional. You get things done and accomplished, which feels good. You plan ahead and do avoid some pitfalls of procrastination. On the other hand, being in control has its downside. It inhibits you from "going with the flow" and seeing where God is trying to steer you. One setback to your schedule makes you scramble to figure out how to get things back on track. The deviation may have been just what God ordered up to steer you in a new direction. The fear, anxiety, and aggravation associated with being in control are debilitating and inhibit growth. We begin seeking our own earthly mission and not our eternal mission, which is far greater and more satisfying. The world will eat you up and leave no leftovers if you let it.

This control mechanism of mine lasted for many years. It was all I knew, and it worked for me. I was ultimately succeeding at life, I thought. I was getting things done, achieving good grades, checking things off the list. What more is there? Let's talk about people for a bit. Family, friendships, romantic relationships...how do they mix with this control factor? Turns out, not great. None of us like to be controlled. I think we all can agree on that. We want to be free to be our own person and make our own decisions.

Controlling because I can't control

Those of us who like to control got this way for different reasons. Maybe that reason is our beginning and the environment we grew up in. Possibly there were too few factors in our control so we started to control things within our grasp. Maybe it was an unhealthy relationship we were in that created a situation where one party was more dominant and we were left feeling inferior and began controlling what we could. Regardless of the reason, control is exhausting! We think things being under our control leads to peace, when in reality, all is not well with our soul. Something is always coming down the pike to throw things off and remind us we are not in control, causing renewed confusion and sending us into a tizzy.

Reflecting back, I know when my control issue began—early in my life at home. My mother was the adult child of an alcoholic. Much pain existed in her home and she felt the effects of it mentally and physically. When she started her own home, she took a huge step in the right direction. No alcohol, no physical abuse; however, the pain of her upbringing lingered. As it ate at her, it spilled out to us. At one time, I could have written a book just on this subject, but now I better understand a truth. Sin causes pain. Pain to ourselves as we carry it daily, and pain to those around us who experience us in a "separated from God" state.

By sin, I refer to any choice we make where a thing, thought, or being becomes more dominant in ordering our decisions than loyalty to our Heavenly Father and His leading.

> *Sin causes pain. Pain to ourselves as we carry it daily, and pain to those around us who experience us in a "separated from God" state.*

My mom was in pain. She hurt so badly.

Well, as a small child living in a home where pain presided, I had two tools in my tool box. Humor and control. I could always find something to joke about. AND...I could always find things to control so that the outcome was better than the emotions swirling around my home.

I didn't always want to let people fully "in" on my life, as it felt like a mess at times. It was not unusual for a fight to erupt and everyone to separate to their corner of the house, uncertain of when we would speak again. Holidays were difficult. Events with emotions involved led to old habits and hurts coming back. One wrong comment and the day was ended.

Sadness and despair reigned often.

So, while Jesus hung on a cross in my home, the parallel of our pain matched that scene. It was heavy. The approach to problem solving then turned either to logic or emotion, not prayer and patience.

I would venture to say that anyone reading this has experienced a time in life when you tried to control things, even if it was not a regular practice. In certain situations, we all do it! What I hadn't learned yet was to turn to Jesus rather than from Him when I was struggling. I went about things alone.

> *The approach to problem solving then turned either to logic or emotion, not prayer and patience.*

As I grew up and left the home, I started to experience life on the outside. People interacted differently than we had as a family, and I didn't know how to have healthy relationships. I didn't allow friendships to develop as deeply as they could. I had too much to do! I valued friends in that I enjoyed social experiences and loved to laugh and have fun, but didn't want to go too deeply in them. As I reflect back, it was almost as if I viewed them as a distraction from my to-do list. That sounds terrible and I am not sure I would have even realized or admitted that at the time, but it has been revealed to me now.

I have a quote on my desk that I wish I would have read and understood 20 years ago! It says: *I used to think that interruptions were annoying, until I realized that interruptions were the job.*

People are interruptions to our daily life. We can either look at them as annoying or messengers from God of something He wants us to know or something we need to do for another. They are an uninvited break that God provides us. How often we turn them away because we think "I've got this, leave me alone." We isolate ourselves from the other sheep in our flock and block out messages from our

Creator. He is trying to break through the hedgerow to us and we keep walking further away. How frustrating that may be for Him! Yet, He keeps sending more sheep after us that may speak in a language that will resonate with us. It may take several sheep or a whole sub-flock, but eventually the lost are found.

> *"And when he comes home, he calls together his friends and his neighbors, saying to them, 'Rejoice with me, for I have found my sheep that was lost.' Just so, I tell you, there will be more joy in heaven over one sinner who repents than over ninety-nine righteous persons who need no repentance."* ~LUKE 15:6-7 (ESV)

I look back now and remember a few sheep that were speaking on behalf of God to awaken me. There were probably many that I don't remember along the way, but that doesn't mean they weren't a vital part of my journey. One sheep lived on my floor sophomore year in college. She was very open with her faith. She was a part of the campus group for Christians and one day came in my room with a conversation about relationships. She had a boy who was interested in her and she drew a diagram for me. She said, "I believe that I am here" and she drew a dot, and God surrounds me. She circled the dot. She continued, "He believes he is here," drawing another dot, "and God is over there," drawing a separate circle on the paper.

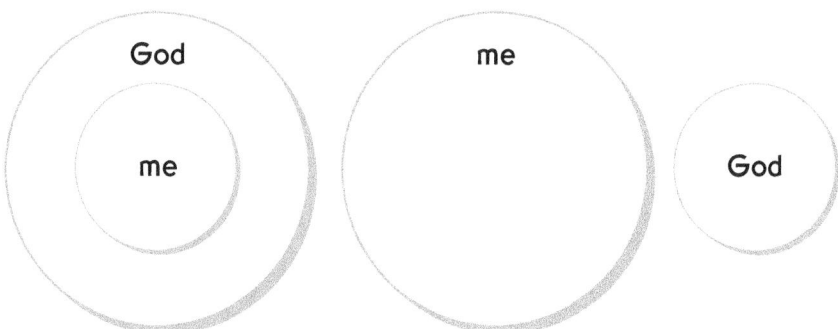

She was illustrating that God was the focus of every aspect of her life and she needed a partner who aligned in that same way. She was years beyond me in faith, and I am embarrassed to say that I thought, "Hmmm, okay." I didn't get it! I guess I was like that guy. I wanted to believe God was the center of my world because it sounded good, but that wasn't how I was living and it definitely wasn't how I was choosing friends or romantic interests. God was nudging me to begin thinking on this.

I had another friend in college tell me once, "Julie, you always say you are fine." I wasn't fine, but again, always wanted to portray I was fine and in control. I never wanted to be a victim or look like I needed help. I suppose I thought that showed weakness or vulnerability. Neither are bad things, but they were things I wanted to avoid feeling in my early years. Being fine and in control are not always traits that allow deep relationships to develop with others. Deep relationships can only develop when you are vulnerable and show weakness. We are asked to do this:

> *Submitting to one another out of reverence for Christ.*
> ~EPHESIANS 5:21 (ESV)

This would have been great advice; however, I was not opening my Bible, did not turn to scripture, and inconsistently attended church at this time in my life. I relied on numero uno, myself. Remember, "I got this."

> *On the outside, I believe I appeared pretty put together.*

An important point to make here is this: on the outside, I believe I appeared pretty put together. I had friends, was doing well in school, socialized. I was "normal." I helped others, talked to others, and believe that most would say I was a good friend. Many times the ways of the world can mask the struggles we have, and we can easily fool others into believing we are "fine" when we really are not. We can build a wall around us, let's say a hedgerow of thorn bushes, so thick that we isolate ourselves to the point that even other lost sheep can't get in. Now, we are in double isolation, struggling, in pain, not allowing help in and becoming our own worst enemy.

Who is Jesus anyway?

Battling the enemy alone is overwhelming. We all need a savior. But Jesus? Who is He anyway? Attempting to understand Jesus is difficult. You try to "understand" Him, put Him in a box and close it. It doesn't fit with the plans you are making.

I am not sure about your background, but I grew up Catholic. In our home, Jesus hung on a cross called a crucifix. If I am honest, He kind of creeped me out (no offense Jesus!). We prayed before meals and bedtime. We attended church on Sundays. Then the dreaded CCD (Confraternity of Christian Doctrine) classes began on Wednesday nights. Throughout my youth I struggled to relate to church, religion, and even Jesus. I learned a lot of ritual but saw church as something I had to do, not something I wanted to do.

As time marched on, I went through first confession. Awkward! I had to sit and tell our priest how much I fought with my sister. Then say the assigned Hail Marys. I had that prayer memorized, but did not appreciate what it meant and forgot what I was doing after a while. First communion then allowed me to get a pretty white dress and receive communion for the first time, along with drinking out of that community wine cup—gross! The blood of Jesus was not on my mind, just catching a contagious illness. Next came 8th grade confirmation. I got a confirmation name, Rose, and had a sponsor. I honestly had no idea what I was doing this for.

As an adult with more maturity and ability to understand the meaning behind these rituals, now I can see the significance, but at the time, I just couldn't grasp the depth of what I was doing. Church was a place to be quiet, solemn, and the figures of Jesus and Mary seemed so sad. I did not equate church or Jesus with joy.

Some of you reading this may really relate. Others may have practiced a different faith, but can still laugh about this. For my non-believers out there, I hope I gave you a chuckle. You have your own reasons for stepping away from God or questioning His existence or significance. It is part of being a caterpillar on a leaf. You can only see so far and understand so much. We can all meet on this truth: there are confusing messages here on Earth about Jesus, our Father, the Holy Spirit, and how God is portrayed in different settings. This confusion can lead us astray, away from our flock if we aren't allowed the freedom and knowledge to explore and understand it.

I can say this, I am very thankful to have had an upbringing acknowledging Jesus, and church being a consistent part of my life. I always had awareness that it was a priority which was an important foundation for me. Thanks Mom and Dad!

Early on, there was a perceived superiority of my faith over protestant churches. This is a bold statement to make, but I am still making it. A vibe that "those" churches weren't doing things right. No one blatantly told me this, it just was there. A strong enough feeling that the freedom to explore other ways of practicing worship was not offered as an option. Almost a polarizing "this way or no way" feeling.

Danger! What if a person grows up in a religious practice they don't relate to? What if the message does not resonate with them, yet they don't feel able to branch out and explore other types of worship? Well, they may find themselves a sheep isolated and turned away from their Creator as earthly rules have been set that took away freedom to make a choice outside of their family practice without judgment. That sheep may then decide it doesn't need church and head off on its own rocky path down the hill away from others. Or worse, the sheep may choose to stop believing altogether. Hopefully, that sheep will consider going rogue, and try something different.

My friends, I feel fortunate; I went rogue and started to make my way through some thorny hedgerows. Get ready for a bumpy ride. I got caught up in a few of them before I made my way through! I had to come to the conclusion that I don't have this on my own.

What is your sin and its cover?

Sin came before us, it is in us, and it is ahead of us. BUT, so is God.

His power is so much stronger than that of sin, and when we allow Him to, He can enable us to conquer the sins within our home. The sins that came before us, have developed within us, and that may occur because of us.

Sin, "an immoral act considered to be a transgression against divine law." In the book of Galatians, it is stated that *"the works of the flesh are evident: sexual immorality, impurity, sensuality, idolatry, sorcery, enmity, strife, jealousy, fits of anger, rivalries, dissensions, divisions, envy, drunkenness, orgies, and things like these."* (5:19-21)

> *"So whoever knows the right thing to do and fails to do it, for him it is sin."* ~JAMES 4:17 (ESV)

Romans goes on to state, *"For all have sinned and fall short of the glory of God."* (3:23)

What about the sin we experience that we did not commit? The pain we feel as a result of others' sin? It seems unfair. It all goes back to the Garden of Eden, that first disobedience to God's command to not eat from a specific tree. One choice affects many. It ripples. At some point, sometimes the origin gets lost and we all start to point fingers at who started the problem. If we look up to our Father as He works within us, we can prevail over sin.

> *"But the Lord is faithful. He will establish you and guard you against the evil one."* ~2 THESSALONIANS 3:3 (ESV)

Sin is an equalizer. No matter the sin, we are committing it together. What I mean by this is that no matter the decision that we make, if it is a decision that does not glorify God and put His will first, we are affecting those around us in a negative way, even if the illusion appears differently. The ripple in the water from every choice spreads far and wide.

BUT, if we can overcome our fear, admitting our sins, we can overcome them together as well. The ripple in the water from these choices spreads far and wide too! These ripples create life and spread truth in a powerful way!

Sometimes I believe we simplify sin to the Ten Commandments and think we are safe if we aren't murdering people or stealing things. Sin goes deeper. In Matthew 5:21-23, it is explained that being angry with a brother is no different than murdering. The intentions of the heart come from the same sin.

> *Something cool happens when we are brave enough to face our sins... they are put into the light where they can shrivel up and DIE!*

I once had a pastor share an image. It was of a large rectangle with the ten commandments around the border. He went on to describe that many people believe they are safe if they live around that border; however, Jesus lies in the center of that rectangle and in order to truly fellowship with Him, we must dig deeper into His commands and see our truth. We must journey into the depths of who we are, where we struggle, and admit our weaknesses. Something cool happens when we are brave enough to face our sins...they are now put into the light where they can shrivel up and DIE! They lose power and control over us. They unite us rather than segregate us. They bring us closer to our flock!

Take a deep breath and acknowledge:

I struggle/fear/find difficult:

_____

Was that difficult?

Now think on this, I struggle/fear/find difficult

_____ and

I justify it or cover it up by

_____.

Congratulations! Speaking your truth took courage. Filling in those blanks catapulted you closer to freedom. You can't be owned by sin that is waving its flag of surrender. What you did my friend is send an SOS signal up to the spiritual realm, and help is on the way!

Get ready to start feeling amazing and free as you become a brand new person!

Today, I surrender:
<u>my secrets</u>.

*Lord, show me
the next step
I must take.*

Chapter 2
Goals & Discussion

What is your "secret" and how are you covering it?

"Therefore, confess your sins to one another and pray for one another, that you may be healed. The prayer of a righteous person has great power as it is working." ~JAMES 5:16

"If we say we have no sin, we deceive ourselves, and the truth is not in us." ~1 JOHN 1:8

We are now in the "Sin" portion of our cycle. The fall began with the apple. What is the sin you struggle with most?

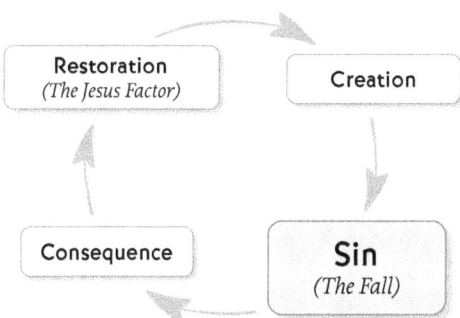

Action Step

Take time to explore your "sin." Draw your circle—where does God stand in your life? At the center, outside, or WAY outside?

1. What is (are) your secret(s)?

2. What are the struggles of your flesh?

   a. Utilize this list from Celebrate Recovery to get you started thinking about where you may need support: *(adult child of dysfunction; anger; chemical dependency; co-dependency; food and body image issues; gambling addiction; love/relationship addiction; mental health; mixed issues; physical, sexual, and emotional abuse; sexual addiction; Veteran PTSD; sexual trauma; or spouse/family transition).*

   b. What steps have you taken, or could you take, to reduce these struggles?

3. How do you "cover" for each sin?

   a. Do you justify it? If so, why and how?

   b. Do you reveal this side of you to others or keep it to yourself?

   c. Do you have success addressing some struggles, but not others? If so, why?

4. Are there people in your life who have hurt you physically or emotionally?

   a. Who?

   b. Have you forgiven them?

   c. How has their pain caused you pain?

5. How have you allowed yourself to be vulnerable with the enemy regarding your sin?

   a. What issues are behind closed doors that you could bring into the light?

   b. Have you taken time to speak with a trusted friend or neutral party to put it into the light?

   c. Have you confessed it to God?

6. Reflect back on your upbringing:

    a. How were the Father, Jesus, and the Holy Spirit depicted in your home?

    b. Did you attend church, and if so what type?

        i. What did you like about it?

        ii. What didn't you like about it?

7. If you are a non-believer, what made you choose this viewpoint, and how did the beginning of your story affect this?

8. What areas of your life do you try to control?

9. Reflect back on people in your life:

   a. Who were sheep directing you back to the flock that you pushed away or ignored?

   b. What messages did God try to get through to you, but you were too in control to hear?

10. What hedgerows have you broken through in your life so far?

    a. Are there others you need to break through to get closer to freedom?

    b. What hedgerows have you built around yourself?

    c. What step could you take right now to approach a hedgerow in your life?

Chapter 3
To My Knees

"If we confess our sins, He is faithful and just to forgive us our sins and to cleanse us from all unrighteousness." ~1 JOHN 1:9 (ESV)

Betrayed.

Alone.

Confused.

Humiliated.

This is the place I sat in after facing the consequence of some of my choices many years ago. It is a lonely place to be when you realize you feel terrible and it was your own fault. Your own choices led you to this place of isolation.

It all started with one poor decision for selfish reasons. I broke a plan with some friends based on fears I had and hope I was putting in a different living situation. I was able to justify my decision, but in that moment, I took a step away from a good flock toward one that was not in alignment with my true purpose, which led me to stray further from my Father and His plans for me.

Once that decision was made, a path was followed that was "not the road less travelled." I chose a path commonly traveled, well worn, with many people on it. What followed was a series of decisions that put my soul in danger. I made friendships not based on the right reasons. I dated someone that I knew I should not. I worked at a location that did not align with my lifestyle.

But, people liked me. I always had somewhere to be. My grades were good. What else could I need?

Reflecting back, clearly I didn't have a true awareness of who I was authentically. Therefore, I was getting tossed by the waves of life.

> *"Then we will no longer be infants, tossed back and forth by the waves, and blown here and there by every wind of teaching and by the cunning and craftiness of people in their deceitful scheming."*
> ~EPHESIANS 4:14

I was living "where" I was, not looking strategically for the people, activities, and environments that would grow me to my highest self. What I have learned is that when we lack that sense of self or God's purpose for our lives, we settle into less than He has planned for us.

> *"For I know the plans I have for you," declares the Lord, "plans to prosper you and not to harm you, plans to give you hope and a future."* ~JEREMIAH 29:11

We should be excitedly running to seek that future, not lying down and accepting where we are. Our lifetime is an opportunity of consistent learning and growth for our soul. Why would God have us here for 70+ years if we stopped spiritually developing once we hit adulthood?

"In fact, though by this time you ought to be teachers, you need someone to teach you the elementary truths of God's word all over again. You need milk, not solid food!" ~HEBREWS 5:12-14

At this point, I was like a baby learning elementary truths. I did not have the knowledge or experience to teach others. I was an adult by our society's standards; however, so juvenile in my spiritual growth. The one great thing was that I was realizing it! I knew I needed to learn more.

I started to awaken.

> *I was running to the wrong place for peace. A peace I would never find in another person.*

I felt alone, confused, scared, and uncertain. I was an avid runner at the time and would go off on a long run and begin to cry, distraught with where my life was personally. It was rough.

My habit had been to call home to be reassured. I began to learn that didn't heal me. It didn't fix my problems. It stirred up more unsettling emotions. I was running to the wrong place for peace. A peace I would never find in another person.

When I found no solution to my pain in people, situations, or circumstances, I finally was right where I needed to be to receive Jesus. Not on the verge of a breakdown, but a breakthrough.

God broke through at the movie theater

During this period, one evening Jesus set up a date for Him and me and I didn't even know it! It was 2004. Mel Gibson co-wrote and directed *Passion of the Christ*.[1] The graphic images changed the trajectory of my life. God spoke to me very directly and sternly in that movie. He invited me in at a time I needed to make a pivotal change in my life. That night, I went home and promised Him from that day forward I would begin to make decisions with more thought of Him in mind. I also began reading a book I had received, The *Purpose Driven Life*[2] by Rick Warren. I was beginning to shed a layer of myself and become more awakened. I changed quite dramatically on the inside. I began attending church consistently. I was hearing the messages in a different way. I was tearing up at the music. I was feeling the Spirit move me in ways I had never felt before. Despite having believed in God and Jesus my entire life, for the first time I was actually becoming a Christian, but I had a long way to go.

I'm a sheep, but still away from my flock

Though realizing that I was a fluffy white sheep, there was a huge hedgerow standing between me and my flock. I had identified my shepherd, now what?

During this time of renewed faith and improving life perspective, I still had many sins, things separating me from God and taking more of my attention. These idols could lead me away from God's intended path for me. Idols such as achievement, social engagements, pride, fears, obligations, desires. One such desire was for a life partnership and this made me vulnerable to the enemy.

> *"Be sober-minded; be watchful. Your adversary the devil prowls around like a roaring lion, seeking someone to devour."* ~1 PETER 5:8 (ESV)

Satan knows our strengths. He knows our weaknesses. He will use them both to tempt us away from our intended path and away from our flock. While our hopes and desires can be used for good, they can also make us vulnerable if we are consumed by them.

I was in recovery. Recovery from a life without Jesus as the center with a lot of hurts and bad habits. I believe I still longed for acceptance, love and belonging. I also had feelings of unworthiness due to the dysfunction in my home and shame associated with that. I was early in the path back to the Lord, and Satan snagged me.

He had been observing my growth and monitoring my weakness. I began a new relationship. The Lord supplied me with an inner-knowing that there were red flags; however, I quieted those truths and listened to the lies of the enemy.

> *It is good enough.*
> *He likes me.*
> *It is the right time.*
> *I am ready for a relationship.*
> *My faith is enough for the two of us.*
> *I need someone in my life.*

Why would I even listen to these lies? **Pain and Fear.**

The **pain** of always longing for a peaceful relationship with someone in which we loved each other and got along. The **fear** of never finding that. The willingness to settle to make it happen.

> *"No temptation has overtaken you that is not common to man. God is faithful, and he will not let you be tempted beyond your ability, but with the temptation He will also provide the way of escape, that you may be able to endure it."* ~1 CORINTHIANS 10:13 (ESV)

God did just what He promised in this verse, He offered me an escape. He offered me at least three different, clear escapes and I shut the door each time. I left myself chained in hell because of fear. Fear that I would hurt someone's feelings. Fear that I was not being loyal by leaving. Fear that I was too far in to turn around now. Fear that I had to face the pain of failing.

LIES.

All of those fears were lies the enemy was feeding into my head and they worked. They worked well. I believed them all. What I had done in my effort to avoid a conflict was to create a greater one. I was not living in my truth. I was not living in God's truth. I was living in fear of living my truth. What a contradiction!

I was a believer in Christ. I was attending church. My conscience was tuned in, but I was not obedient. I had one other major battle I was fighting: I was isolated. I did not have a flock of believers to challenge, love, or support me. I was alone with the enemy and another lost sheep. We were far from the flock, in need of a shepherd.

New believer danger

Going to your knees is an exciting moment. A pivotal life change. It is also one of the most dangerous phases as a believer. I believe it is one where you are most at risk of the enemy steering you away. When you begin to *see*, everything starts to light up in color. Something else lights up, awareness of your flaws!

Take extreme caution. The enemy can even use your belief against you. He can fill you with lies that you are unworthy. He will remind you of all your wrongs. He will make your life change seem impossible. He will even cloud God's Word at times, twisting it to keep you enslaved to him.

It is vital when you are awakened and start heading back towards the flock to grab another believer to walk with. The wolf is out there prowling and he is angry. He just lost another one. Don't let him snag you from your divinely lit path.

So, here is what I did friends: I settled into a life that wasn't meant for me. A life that wasn't serving anyone or anything, but fear. I had every warning in the book, but I wasn't wise enough or experienced enough in my faith to take appropriate action to keep everyone safe. I was a lone sheep behind a huge hedgerow of thorn bushes.

I was a new believer in danger, but God…

Today, I surrender:
my fear.

*Lord, show me
the next step
I must take.*

Chapter 3
Goals & Discussion

What are your fears?

"Fear not, for I am with you; be not dismayed, for I am your God; I will strengthen you, I will help you, I will uphold you with my righteous right hand." ~ISAIAH 41:10 (ESV)

Our story is now in the "Consequence" portion of our cycle. What has resulted from the sin in your life?

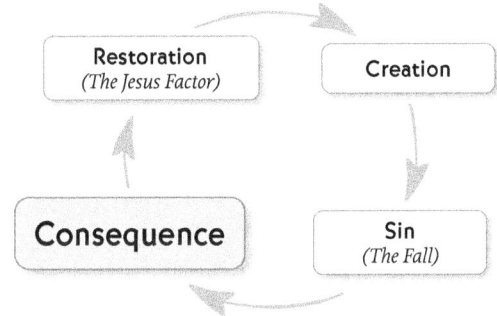

Action Step

Questions to ponder:

1. What is/are your fear(s)?

    a. Have you taken action on any of them?

    b. Why haven't you taken action on the remaining ones?

2. What events in your life have taken you to your knees to re-evaluate how you are living or what direction you are going?

    a. Have you taken action as a result?

3. What messages in society have pulled you closer to God or pushed you further from him?

4. Has God offered you an escape from a troublesome situation, but you weren't willing or did not know the direction to go so you stayed where you were?

    a. Are you still conflicted with whether to make that change?

    b. Did anything positive come from staying and not making the change?

    c. Do you see the escape route more clearly right now?

5. Could you be in "new believer danger"?

   a. Who could you speak with about being your partner sheep as you walk back to the flock?

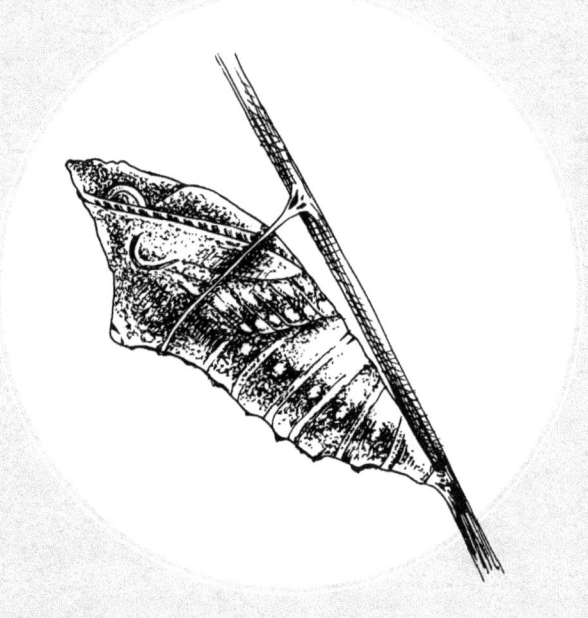

Part 2
The Chrysalis

As we progress through this life, if we are fortunate, we begin to acknowledge our need for something more. That is God calling us to come home. That acknowledgement sends us into the chrysalis of His protection as we begin our transformation process. Just as the threads of God that have connected all of the people we have encountered and our experiences, the caterpillar creates a chrysalis around itself. All of those experiences wrap around us preparing us for the next step. Our view remains of little color inside those tightly bound threads. We are learning we need instruction, but inconsistently listening and waiting to act. We are vulnerable to the enemy attack as we are not fully aware of ourselves and are still learning our strengths and weaknesses. The good news is our strength is increasing as our support and flock is growing! Our wings are starting to develop as we prepare to emerge....

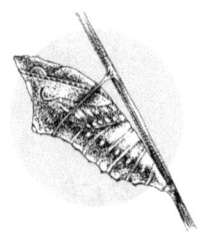

Chapter 4
Finding Fellowship

"Therefore encourage one another and build one another up, just as you are doing." ~1 THESSALONIANS 5:11 (ESV)

Path chosen.

Escape route declined.

Keep moving forward.

Despite making choices that God may not prefer, He never leaves us. He always runs up ahead to keep gently steering us back. He met me where I was, amidst my pain, struggles, and decisions, in a small town church.

Raised Catholic, I was a bit rogue to start testing out Protestant churches, but my heart was open to find God in a new place. My husband and I had just moved and there were two churches in town, just down the road in fact—a Christian church and a Mennonite church. Knowing nothing about Mennonites, I thought, "How cool if this

Christian church was a good fit and I could literally walk to church each Sunday." I checked it out and while a nice church, I didn't feel a connection. A couple months later, I decided to try the Mennonite church. Worst case scenario, these people are weird and I just won't go back ☺. I walked in and was greeted by what would be my spiritual family for the next nine most formative years of my journey back to Jesus. It was such a genuine group of true believers. I felt at home and comforted.

A clearing in the hedgerow of thorn bushes that had developed in my life revealed a flock of sheep on the other side. After moving to a new town, I was searching for a church home to be a part of and found a community of believers that could share the passion that was developing in me for God. I had never experienced fellowship. I had not experienced the closeness of a church family. I didn't get it. In the past I went to church and left as quickly as I came, and went back to my life.

In the past I went to church and left as quickly as I came, and went back to my life.

In his book, Rick Warren states, "Your spiritual family is even more important than your physical family because it will last forever." Having come from a family with broken relationships and struggles for peace, I longed for this. I was finding my brothers and sisters in Christ who offered me genuine love. It felt so good!

It didn't take long for one of God's special sheep to journey my way and pull me in close. Her name was Rose.

Rose

Rose was the kind of woman every person needs in their life. She would greet you and "see" you in a way that she would never forget you and you would never forget her. She committed to her relationship with you and grabbed your hand saying, "We will do this together." I was still learning the church when I came home one day and a baby shower invitation was taped to my door. Rose had found my home and hand delivered this invitation to make sure I felt included for this upcoming shower. I didn't even know the mom (she is now a close friend). At first I didn't know what to think. I had never seen this type of outreach and wasn't sure if I should be touched or run away, figuratively speaking.

> Sometimes the light of our Father is so bright that when we have been living in the dark, we are blinded by it and take a step back.

It is sad how sometimes when God shows us love through others, it is so foreign at first to us that we turn from it. Sometimes the light of our Father is so bright that when we have been living in the dark, we are blinded by it and take a step back.

I didn't attend that baby shower, but Rose continued to build a relationship with me. She took time to get to know me and shine her light onto me week after week. She quickly became the closest I had gotten to Jesus here on Earth. She was a magnifying glass of His love and goodness. The most Godly Christian woman I had encountered on a personal level in my life.

She poured her gifts into the church. One of her biggest was Christmas decorations! The church was decorated in such a special way at Christmas with every last detail accounted for. I learned that Rose would spend countless hours at the church rearranging and adding décor all through the holiday season so that it was as special as if it was her own home. I would venture to say even more special than her own home. She loved Jesus and it showed!

I spent those first few years at the church soaking it in. Observing and watching the magic happen in the congregation, appreciating their fellowship, and having a spiritual family I could count on week after week that would support my faith and me as a person on this journey of life.

I was invited to attend Sunday school, but didn't dive in immediately. I still didn't attend every Sunday as my husband wasn't all in on the church thing and I wavered in my loyalty to God in this area. There was never judgment for missing a Sunday, just a warm welcome the next visit. Church became a pleasant experience for me. The prayers felt genuine and real. The people felt genuine and real. I felt God had led me to this wonderful family to help me in my faith journey back to Him. A family that would gently pull me in close until I was so tightly in their flock that I was safe from the other side of the hedgerow in which I had been living.

Death

About four years after my being a part of the best kept secret in my new small town, Rose passed away. She fought a great battle against cancer and never lost her faith or her smile. One memory of her that is most significant to me happened not long before she passed. It changed me forever. My husband had sustained a debilitating injury. We had a one-year-old. Income had dramatically decreased. Emotions were high and low. Amidst Rose's own battle against cancer, she called to check on me one night. Me. What followed her phone call was the most genuine act of kindness I had experienced to that point in my life. Rose planned an evening, prepared a hot meal, and delivered it in beautiful dishes on a serving tray ready to eat. Her body was weak at this point and she could barely pull it from the car. It was delicious. Pork chops, Asian salad, and mashed

> *What followed her phone call was the most genuine act of kindness I had experienced to that point in my life.*

potatoes. I can taste it now. What a servant of the Lord. The truth is, I should have been taking her a meal!

Rose's death impacted me so deeply. I had never grieved a physical loss of someone I cared for before. I longed to read the encouraging notes she had sent, hear the sweet sound of her voice, and spot her outside when I took a walk. She was gone. The closest I had been to Jesus, taken away.

I made a decision after Rose's death. I needed to honor her for who she was in my life. I needed to go all in as a servant of the Lord so that I might have the impact on others that she had on me. I began to use my gifts at church and in the community. I looked for opportunities to encourage others. I became more than a seat-warmer at church.

Rose's death resurrected my servant heart. A chainsaw had just cut a huge hole in that hedgerow of thorn bushes and pulled me right through, blocking the entrance so that I would be safe until I realized on my own the power of the Holy Spirit within me!

I found my flock!

Today, I surrender:
my isolation.

*Lord, show me
the next step
I must take.*

Chapter 4
Goals & Discussion

Has God called you to a flock?

"Therefore encourage one another and build one another up, just as you are doing." ~1 THESSALONIANS 5:11

And now our story is in the "Restoration" portion of our cycle. How has God tried to restore you, your situation, and your life after the consequences that resulted from a sinful choice?

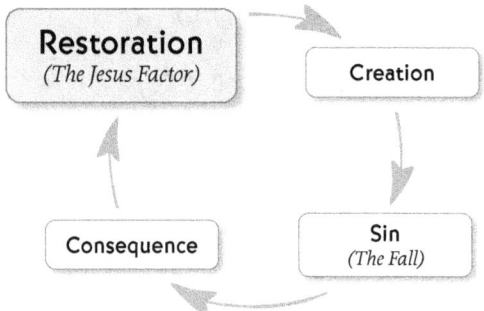

Action Step

Questions to ponder:

1. Have you experienced fellowship in your life?

    a. If yes, what do you enjoy about it?

    b. If no, what church experience are you currently having?

2. Who has positively impacted your church experiences and why?

3. Who has negatively impacted your church experience and why?

4. Are you contributing your gifts to the church and community you are a part of?

   a. If yes, what are they?

   b. If no, what holds you back from investing more of yourself into your church and community?

5. Is church participation something you do to meet a requirement or obligation? If so, why?

   a. If no, why is church something you don't find necessary?

6. How would you define yourself?

  a. Independent sheep

  b. Part of a flock

   - Is your flock helping or inhibiting your growth?

   - Do you believe God led you to your flock or that you chose your own?

  c. Heading towards the flock

   - Who helped to find you?

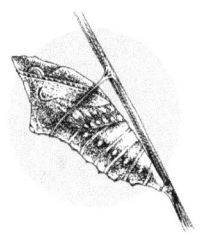

Chapter 5

Rylie

"And God breathed new life into me"

"See, I am doing a new thing! Now it springs up; do you not perceive it? I am making a way in the wilderness and streams in the wasteland." ~ISAIAH 43:19

When Jesus restores you, a new creation begins within you and from you. Creation can look different for all of us. It may be a new pet for one or inspiration in a project that has hit a stopping point for others. For me, it was a child.

I was at 39 weeks and 1 day pregnant, feeling worn down and tired, when I trudged to work for another day. I hadn't been at work but 30 minutes when I felt an odd gush. That fear of my water breaking in a public setting was coming to life. Thank goodness for being an over-prepared, first-time pregnant woman—I had packed towels in the car! I arrived at the hospital around 9:00 AM and welcomed little Rylie at 11:53 AM. I remember it like it was yesterday.

I was thirty years old when I gave birth to my son Rylie. The truth is, this book began after Rylie's birth when God was making Himself very real in my life. So real, the Spirit was compelling me to journal my experiences to share with others. God brought me to life through Rylie. Bundle of Joy…what an understatement! When you receive a child as the gift they truly are, they will bring you an intimate level of joy that only God can provide.

I had found my flock, but suddenly had a "to my knees" moment. As I sat on maternity leave soaking in my little one and processing the transformative change that was taking place in my life, God was speaking to me. He took this opportunity when I was aware and listening and spoke clearly to me. I had been re-reading *The Purpose Driven Life*, by Rick Warren and something triggered me to recall someone with whom I needed to make amends. I realized someone in my life had offered me a tremendous amount of grace and I had never acknowledged it, apologized, or appreciated it. I had simply moved on. I was getting a strong nudge to contact this friend and admit my wrongs and make amends.

Apology or remorse?

Forgiveness was hard to come by in my home growing up. Often a hurt happened followed by…silence.

Would the silence last for hours, days, a week? It depended on the depth of the hurt. That hurt ran back a lifetime before mine. It wasn't what occurred that day. As a child, I wanted peace in my home. I always tried to bring everyone together to make things right, but the healing required was much deeper than anything I could accomplish or understand. We needed Jesus. He was close, but we had not accessed Him to the fullest.

I learned to move on. Grace and forgiveness were strangers to me.

When you tend to control things, feeling remorse or apologizing can be difficult. Taking that a step further, sincerely apologizing and meaning it is even more difficult. Another admission of weakness on your part, and owning that is painful. That is saying you did something wrong which is not on your to-do list, and it means you misstepped. That can throw you into a quandary, questioning yourself and admitting defeat.

> *"Therefore, confess your sins to one another and pray for one another, that you may be healed. The prayer of a righteous person has great power as it is working."* ~JAMES 5:16 (ESV)

The danger here again is isolation. If we are interacting with one another, we are going to have disagreements. We are going to offend one another at times and differ in opinion. If we are unable to get vulnerable and admit remorse or apologize to maintain healthy relationships, we limit ourselves from the beautiful gift we have been given in loving one another. We instead look at others with judgment, isolate ourselves, and judge ourselves as well. This behavior is a dangerous breeding ground for the enemy to do his deadliest work. Rather than be vulnerable with God and his people, we let ourselves get vulnerable with the enemy behind closed doors where nothing good happens.

> *If we are unable to get vulnerable to maintain healthy relationships, we limit ourselves from the beautiful gift we have been given in loving one another.*

Step 8 in Celebrate Recovery[1] states, "We made a list of all persons we had harmed and became willing to make amends to them all. *'Do to others as you would have them do to you. Luke 6:31'*"

As I thought about the friend that I had offended, tears streamed down my face. Obediently, I grabbed a card and began to write and write. The Spirit led me to get it all out, everything she needed to know. All the words I needed to express to cleanse her and me of the situation in our past. I was scared. This had occurred several years prior. We had "successfully" moved on and were cordial with one another; however, I strongly felt God telling me that this needed to happen. Unaware of "Step 8" at the time, I now know this was a part of my recovery as a non-Christian becoming a Christian. I needed to do this to move forward in my faith. As important, she needed to know this to grow her own faith and realize the great work she was doing for her Father.

> *When God enters the picture to restore us, new life is created in and from us.*

I got that opportunity to give my note to her. Although she had already forgiven me and moved on like a true child of God, something had healed in her. I was thankful God had awakened me and encouraged me to do this. She deserved it and it grew my faith. It also did something else. It empowered me to be prepared to offer grace to another, many others.

When God enters the picture to restore us, new life is created in and from us. Rylie was new life that awakened me to God's greatness. It also inspired me to give "life," by being more loving to others. These acts also "created." Love creates life!

> *"A person's words can be life-giving water; words of true wisdom are as refreshing as a bubbling brook."* ~PROVERBS 18:4 (NLT)

A domino effect happened. God gave me life physically and spiritually. Rylie was a physical creation of life, but He also created a new me in the process. He inspired me to speak life to a friend which further inspired me to offer grace to a different friend which in turn spoke life to her.

Now that is a thinker!

It all started with God's love and grace. He trusted me with that amazing creation of Rylie and I praise Him for that. He woke me up and my life started to get new meaning. Black and white began to fade and color started to enter the picture.

Cue butterflies, rainbows, and sunshine!

Online shopping, a storm, and a little boy

The Life God had breathed into me was exhilarating. It was as if I was living for the first time. I was seeing, hearing, and feeling everything differently. I began appreciating aspects of my life I never had before. Even more importantly, I was realizing God was taking a chance on imperfect me to take care of an amazing creation He breathed life into. It was a privilege and I didn't want to let Him down! Then God gave me a little view into his omniscience and blew me away!

Fall was fast approaching and my 18-month-old needed cool weather clothes. If you have children, you know how that works. You purchase one season of clothes and as they outgrow those clothes, you have to purchase an entirely new wardrobe to last through the next season. As a full-time working mom, shopping wasn't on my top list of priorities since time was of the essence and I tried to maximize as much quality time with my son as I could. We were working on one income due to my husband's injury and were not looking for reasons to spend money.

One day in October, I received a Kohl's coupon. I got those almost weekly it seemed, and often discarded them as I was not looking for a reason to buy something. This time was different. I thought, "Maybe I could use this to get my son his new fall wardrobe and save some money at that. Better yet," I thought, "I can shop online; this way I don't have to leave the house, I can save gas, and do it while my son is napping. PERFECT!" I jumped online and started to browse. Online shopping can be dangerously easy! I found everything I needed and more to get us through the cool months: pants, long-sleeved shirts, hat, mittens, coat, and socks. I was getting some great deals! I went to my shopping cart to purchase and came to the section where I could enter my coupon promotional code. I peeled the sticker and had 30% off, yippee! WAIT, the coupon wasn't valid for several more days. Frustrated, I wondered if I could call customer service and perhaps be able to apply my coupon anyway.

The Kohl's customer service representative answered and listened politely to my problem. She said, "Well, I can't help you apply the 30% discount, but I can apply an old 15% discount for which I have a promotional code." I thought for a minute and accepted the offer. It was better than no discount. I already found EVERYTHING I wanted and many items were significantly discounted already. Ahhh, done! It is such a relief to know you have purchased what you needed and saved money at that!

A few days later, I received the familiar "your purchase is being sent" email. However, something odd I noticed, I had two of them. I almost hit delete thinking it was just a duplicate (as they often can be), but something in me told me to look at both.

Oh no! I was getting the SAME order twice! One at the original pricing before any discounts and one at the 15% discounted price. The customer service representative must have entered the order a second time rather than replacing the existing order with the 15% discount. I called the number in the email immediately to stop the full price order from being sent. I was greeted with an "It is too late." What? I am calling before the order is sent; you can save shipping and handling. "No, you will have to just accept the order and return it in the store." I was a bit frustrated.

Not too long after I got off of the phone I thought, "Hmm, I think I was supposed to get these extra clothes for a reason. I will just select several items and donate them to Operation Christmas Child." I had planned on packing a shoebox with my son already and I was meant to get these items to send to another little boy. I was now at peace with this error and moved on with my day.

When I arrived home that night, I explained the scenario to my husband. Mind you, we were living pretty much paycheck to paycheck, so bringing up the idea of donating several items in this duplicate order seemed a little odd to him, but he humored me. When the second order arrived, I selected the items I wanted to donate, a coat, hat, mittens, long-sleeved top, pants, and socks; almost a full outfit for an 18–24 month boy minus shoes. That should help out a boy in need I thought. I put the items in my closet and gathered the rest of the items to return to Kohl's when I had some spare time.

Messages from God

Soon after this event, I was triggered to read a passage out of *Our Daily Bread*,[2] those little booklets you get at church. The message for the day I was reading was "Give when you have nothing to give." Boy, I sure felt we had not much to give financially. I always try to give anyway, but sometimes I am nervous to give generously...uncomfortably.... This message inspired me even more to continue my current plan of donating these clothes to a little boy. So, I believed I was on the right path.

Later that evening, I got on my email and noticed I had Kohl's cash sitting there. One set for the first order and one for the second order. "Hmm, what if I return the entire second order, and re-purchase the items I want to donate and save some money with the Kohl's cash." In a weird way I thought God was drawing me to this email to help me out financially. It was as if God was saying, *"Thanks for listening to my request, now save yourself a little more money while you do this favor for me."* I took off for Kohl's not long after concocting my plan, waiting in line, and reached the customer service desk. The man behind the counter empathized with my order confusion, returned the items, and let me re-purchase with my Kohl's cash. Now get this, next he let me apply that 30% coupon I had that I wasn't able to use because I was too early. Well, now it wasn't.

I had to just look up to God and say, "Really, you are trying to save me more money again." It was at that moment that something very powerful came over me. God was working overtime to get these 18-24 months boys' clothes to a little boy in need. I no longer was thinking of me and what I needed to do, but about this unknown little boy that God was using me to help out. I felt a rush of adrenaline course through my body. There are few times in my life that I have realized God was using me in such a way as this time. As I drove home, I said a prayer with everything in my being, "God, I know you are using me to get clothes to some little boy in need. Please let me know who that little boy is. I will wait for your instructions." I got home and put those clothes in my closet again. I knew God would let me know when I needed to do something with them.

That evening, I visited the Operation Christmas Child website. I now had my items I wanted to send; however, something wasn't right. Again, I had a strong feeling that this is not where the clothes were to be sent. Maybe they would end up going to a country where winter clothes weren't needed. Whatever the reason, I knew I needed to stop in my tracks. There was some little boy right here that needed these clothes. I went down the hall to tell my husband these synchronicities I was experiencing and he listened, but I could tell he thought I was a little out there.

Not long after this, I opened another devotional I was reading at the time, one I had on interlibrary loan: *Heaven Changes Everything.*[3]

If you have heard of *Heaven is for Real*, well, this was a follow up to that book but written in the form of a devotional. That night, the passage I happened to open was about "Giving when you have nothing to give." This is a little eerie I thought. Boy, God sure was hitting me over the head with this message. I even laughed and said, "I get it God." I plan to give. After reading this second passage though, I realized that God really wanted me paying attention to this donation. He had plans for it and I needed to listen carefully to his instructions. So, I waited, patiently! This was difficult for me. I prefer to check things off the list, clear the space. To leave a pile of items and wait challenged me. I needed to donate these clothes when the timing was right, according to God's plan.

The next few days at work, I shared my story with a few close friends who share a strong faith. I thought they would be interested in this story and not think I was completely crazy. I felt so exuberant about what I was experiencing. God's power was running through me and I felt so honored. One co-worker of mine came down to my office for a work-related question. I asked her if she was a believer. She answered with tears that came to her eyes, "I feel angry with God right now," she said. That strong feeling that God was channeling through me came over me again. It felt as if God put her right in front of me at that particular moment to share this story and possibly re-ignite her faith. She continued to explain why her faith had been shaken: a recent traumatic death of a family member and her son's estrangement from her and his involvement in some questionable things. I listened and at the appropriate timing shared my story. She listened and laughed and we moved on with our day.

> *God's power was running through me and I felt so honored.*

The storm

Several days, maybe a week or more went by. It was a Sunday and the weather was nasty that day. The temperature was oddly warm for that time of year and the wind was so strong it blew one of our screens off. We headed off to church and heard tornado sirens were going off in other towns. Fortunately, our town wasn't affected too badly—some tree limbs down, and other wind damage, but nothing major. We were heading to a couples' book club that day where we focused on faith-based marriage type books. They lived in a nearby town where the power was out. As I packed up my son's bag, something made me reach into one of the front pockets. "Oh my gosh, Donkey!" That lone piece that fits into our Bible animals' book was found! I had been looking for it for six months and had no luck. I had given up and here it was, in a pocket I knew I had scoured a million times before today. My senses heightened. Again, I felt that God was saying, "Get ready." "Am I crazy?" I thought. "Jesus did ride into Jerusalem on a donkey that had never been ridden before." I didn't share this part of my story with too many people because I kind of thought I would sound like a kook, but inside, I knew to be ready!

> *This was what God had been preparing me for, the time was now.*

We had our book club discussion and headed home. Shortly after returning home, we turned on the news and learned that another nearby town had been completely devastated by the storm that day. My adrenaline was pumping, I felt anxious, I knew! I looked at my husband and said, "That is where the clothes are supposed to go." This was what God had been preparing me for, the time was now and I needed to again wait until the little boy in need of these clothes surfaced. It was so clear. There was no more guessing.

I was not on social media, but my husband was. Now I was on a mission. I asked my husband if he saw or heard anything about a little boy in need of clothes to alert me. We had to have all ears ready to learn of the boy in need of the clothes God had asked me to save for him. I went to work the next day and of all days, my husband had to stop by to get the carrier out of my car to pick up our son. When he stopped, he said, "Hey, a family that works with our friend lost everything in the storm. They are taking donations and have three kids." "Okay," I said, "I will email her and see what ages the kids are." Is this it? Is God about to reveal this special little boy? I sent an email and said, "I heard about the need for items for your co-worker's family. Does she have a little boy that would fit into 18–24 months clothes? I waited and waited. That evening, she replied back YES!

I started buzzing around the house like a bee. I came out and told my husband, "I found him, I found him. The little boy has been revealed." I began to pack up my bag of items to deliver to my friend the next morning. I thought, why stop here, this family lost EVERTYHING! So, I started adding things; I added blankets, towels, rags, toiletries, stuffed animals, a gift card to eat out , and more.

Again, I felt God speak to me. I strongly felt He wanted me to let this family and specifically this little boy know how much He loved him and how hard He worked to help him long before the storm ever came. So I sat down and wrote and wrote. I told him that he must be a special little boy with a special family. God was watching over them and working hard for them behind the scenes even if they didn't realize it. I didn't know who to address the envelope to, so I decided to put an inspirational message on the front. I opened my devotional that was on interlibrary loan again to a page for which I no longer have the exact scripture. It was about how scary the world can be, but if you imagine yourself sitting in Jesus' lap that you will feel better. Perfect!

Oh, one last note, that evening as I lay down in bed, I grabbed that devotional that had inspired me twice during these events. As I opened the front cover, I noticed something I hadn't paid attention to before. Remember, I had it on interlibrary loan; it had a library stamp from the same town as the storm. Now, I checked this book out weeks before any of these events occurred. I think this was one of the first clues that God knew what was coming.

I delivered the items to my friend the next morning and asked, "So what is this little boy's name?" She said Dawson.

The story is complete or is it?

I drove on to work and was trembling from this experience. The story was finished. One of my first thoughts was, I can't wait to share this story with those who I started it with, especially my co-worker who had begun to lose her faith. As I stepped out of my car in the parking lot, I turned around and she was standing right there. It was almost as if God planted her there because He wanted her to hear something to renew her faith. Not almost, He did plant her there—I know it! As we walked in, I said, "You won't believe it," and she stopped me and said, "You found your little boy?" I said "yes." It brings tears to my eye even today. I continued to tell her the story and thought, *this story isn't over.* God is still working; He just knows He has my attention now to wait for His next instruction. I looked up to Him and said, "You are good!"

Revelations

This series of events was so moving to me it is hard to describe. I have been growing more and more in my faith for the last several years. I have always believed in God, Jesus, and the Holy Spirit, but I feel I developed a relationship with God not too long ago in my early twenties. I was brought to my knees and had to look at my life, my decisions, my friends, and everything to figure out how to get back on track. I truly began to fall in love with God and what He had to offer. I started to listen. But I was still immature in my relationship with God, so I don't know that I heard everything He wanted me to hear at all times. Nonetheless, I felt very close with God and was very sure that He held the answers to an abundant life and our purpose here on Earth.

Something significant happened when this story was revealed. I realized a few things that I think I already knew but were now shown to me clearly:

1. God is working through other people even when we don't know He is.
2. God motivates others to pray for us in time of need even if we don't have the strength to pray, know what to pray for, or realize we need to pray.
3. God truly knows what is going to happen and prepares us for it and has plans to help us through whatever comes our way.
4. God wants to excite us about His presence in our lives so that we share it with others and renew or spark their faith as well as our own.
5. If we listen to God's instructions, He will give us the tools we need to complete his work.
6. **Be patient** and wait for God's instructions!

Waiting for instructions from God

The strongest message I got through this entire experience was to "wait for God's instructions." I was so tuned in to God during this process that with bated breath I waited to learn my next step. This made me start wondering how many other times I missed out on wonderful opportunities to do God's

How many other times I missed...

work because I didn't listen, I moved too fast or at my own pace to get something done, or because I simply didn't turn to God to ask for guidance in a scenario. I have learned that God wants us to turn to him in all that we do, not just the big stuff!

I have a good friend who shares a strong faith in God. She told me once that she had either heard or read a story: A mother talked to her daughter one day about having a relationship with God. She said, "When do you pray?" and the daughter replied, "Oh, for the big stuff, not for things like passing a test or something." The mom replied by saying, "Would you only tell a best friend the big stuff, or would you tell them all of the small stuff you are dealing with too?" Wow, what a great way to describe a healthy relationship with God. We should take EVERYTHING to God, not just the big stuff. He wants to know about every joy, concern, fear, things that make us angry or sad, things that make us feel insecure or inadequate, things that make us bitter, things that make us happy.

With each prayer or thought, we are allowing God to be present in our lives; we are focusing on Him and allowing Him to work in us. We are taking an opportunity to re-direct ourselves to the path He wants us on, rather than rushing through our day at our own pace on our own agenda. We should work at God's pace, according to God's agenda, and GREAT things will happen! Remember, it all comes back to "Waiting for God's Instructions!"

God's instructions lead to creation of new life!

Today, I surrender:
my path.

*Lord, show me
the next step
I must take.*

Chapter 5
Goals & Discussion

Has God provided a new pathway for you?

> *"See, I am doing a new thing! Now it springs up; do you not perceive it? I am making a way in the wilderness and streams in the wasteland."* ~ISAIAH 43:19

Our story has returned to the "Creation" portion of our cycle. How has God created new in your life?

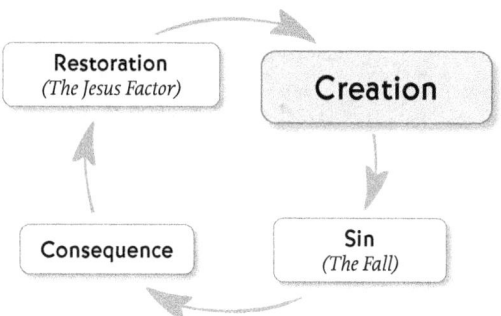

Action Step

Questions to ponder:

1. Has God presented any new pathway(s) to you?

2. What transformative experiences in your life have you had to date?

   a. What about each experience was transforming?

   b. What changes in yourself resulted from this experience?

3. Are there experiences in your life that could have been transformative, but you held yourself back from the experience due to fear or confusion?

   a. What ways could you allow that experience to transform you now as you reflect on it?

   b. What action steps could you take to further your transformation related to that experience now? (You may have hit pause, but you can hit play at any time. ☺)

4. Have you received grace from someone? Have you told them thank you?

    a. Have you given grace to someone as a result of receiving grace?

    b. Did you tell the TRUE original grace giver (our Father) thank you?

    c. Is there someone who needs your grace right now?

5. Are there people in your life with whom you need to have a conversation around an apology, showing remorse, or a need to clear the air?

    a. If so, who? What is stopping you from having that discussion today?

Take the step!

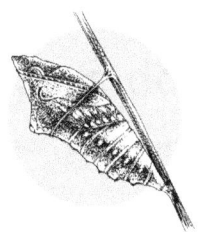

Chapter 6
Pressure is Mounting

*"I am bent over and racked with pain.
All day long I walk around filled with grief."* ~PSALM 38:6 (NLT)

Sin leads to pain. Pain in our body. Pain in our mind. Pain spiritually as we turn from our Father.

The minute we make a choice that does not align with who we are meant to be, we know it. We feel it, deep inside. We are faced with a choice. Admit the mistake. Face the problem head on. Say our apology if needed. Back up and start over.

OR, shove that pain deep down and keep moving forward, convincing ourselves it will work out.

Remember when I went *to my knees* in Chapter 3? I was faced with a temptation and avoided my escape route. I pushed down that pain and moved on. I moved far along that alternate path I chose. I got married on that path. I had a child on that path. Life "looked" good.

However, deep inside my body, my sin, my choice that disregarded our Father's will for my life, could no longer be hidden.

Stabbing pain

Once my son was born, I started really noticing a stabbing and burning pain in my upper right muscle near the shoulder. It didn't surprise me with all that is involved with a newborn: breastfeeding every 1 to 2 hours, no sleep, holding a baby throughout the day while you multi-task on daily duties. All of these activities could contribute to some body aches for sure. This pain had been there prior to having my son, but I definitely noticed it had worsened.

When I started back to work at a primarily desk job, the pain continued to intensify. Sometimes I could get no relief and tried stretching my arm around in all different ways to feel some decrease in the pain, but nothing quite worked. Yoga, stretching, massage—nothing cured the pain. When my son was about 9 months old, I visited a good friend who happened to be a chiropractor. His wife was one as well. He suggested I go to a chiropractor. I thought, "But my back seems fine." I didn't want to accept that I would need to start seeing a chiropractor and begin a regular regimen of visits. So I put it off and went back to my natural remedies of yoga, stretching, and icing at night. This was easy and in my *comfort zone.*

The pain continued, but I did my best to ignore it. Life was too busy to stop for this. I didn't want to appear to be a whiner or weak. Fast forward 5 to 6 months and I got desperate again. I decided to get a massage. It was extremely painful, but in a good way! ☺ The massage therapist said I had a real problem in that upper right muscle near my shoulder. She ended up working on it the entire time and suggested I come back. She also asked to do a new technique on me called Reiki. I had never heard of it so she explained that it involved placing her hands on the area needing attention, to support my healing. "Okay. It can't hurt," I thought. I experienced a stillness I had not experienced in a long time. No touch, just me and God. He had me still...and was calling me to awaken further to learn the source of my pain.

A couple more months went by and we had our friends, the chiropractors, down for Thanksgiving. While we ate our meal, I started talking about that pain again because it was really affecting me that night. Again, my friend asked me several questions, made his unofficial diagnosis of me and told me how he would treat me if I were seeing him. He followed up a couple weeks later with an email and asked, "Have you called the chiropractor yet?" I admitted I had not, so he suggested I at least check with my insurance to see what coverage I had. I did and I had pretty good coverage. He was able to suggest a few chiropractors in my area and one was conveniently located by my office and seemed like a good fit. By the first week in December, I had my appointment scheduled.

Stepping into new territory

The chiropractor office was very inviting, but definitely different than any other medical office I had ever been to. There was a different mindset here than I was accustomed to and I found myself out of my *comfort zone* again. Now, believe me, being a Registered Dietitian, I can appreciate these naturopathic ways of thinking, but it was a new way to "treat" my body. I still hoped I wouldn't have permanent nerve damage with a manipulation and that I wouldn't pass gas while she adjusted me, ha! Laugh if you wish, but this was a big hold up for me to go!

The doctor came in and met me and explained the chiropractor philosophy. It made sense. By getting your spine back into alignment, you help your body to function in a better state and heal itself. Somewhat like a physical alignment to your "truth." As a Registered

Dietitian and a previous wellness champion in my workplace, I am all about embracing ways of living healthfully.

The next step was to get x-rays for some initial goals for my plan of care to see what was really causing this pain. They took several images to get my entire neck and spine. The next week was my first adjustment, and I was nervous! When I arrived, we went through the x-rays and I had a reasonable case of scoliosis that could definitely benefit from some adjusting. My chiropractor realized that the lowest part of my spine was cut off in the last x-ray and said they got a pretty good picture of what was going on, but if I was willing, she would like to get one more x-ray at the bottom for a full picture. My insurance would fully cover this, so I agreed to it. We did the x-ray, and I got my first adjustment. I survived (without any embarrassing moments)!

> *I was learning how to invest time into my health and wellness and it took work and commitment to realign in this way.*
>
>

As I got used to this new schedule of adjustments three times a week, I had to modify my work schedule to make it happen. On top of that, I had a short window to get this done and get to daycare on those days to pick up my son. I can't say I was too "relaxed" that first week as I got used to this. One day while sitting there, I saw the clock ticking away closer to the time I needed to be on the road to get my son, and the office was a little backed up. I was learning how to invest time into my health and wellness and it took work and commitment to realign in this way (pun intended).

I went in for a series of adjustments and quickly noticed an improvement in my pain. For days I would have no pain at all. It was exciting. I also returned for massage and reiki treatments.

I was choosing to be still more often.

I was investing in myself: mind and body.

God was reaching me in new ways and helping me unravel my emotional pain. It was time to dig to the root of my surface level aches and pains.

A twist

I knew this would be a process and I would need to keep at it to make headway, but so far, so good. After about a week, I arrived at the office for a scheduled adjustment and was placed in a consultation room. "I wonder why they put me in here?" Soon, the doctor arrived and started going through my x-rays again. I was thinking, "Why are we doing this again..." Then, she arrived at the last x-ray I had taken and dropped a bomb on me. The radiologist who reviewed the x-ray was concerned. There was an area of my intestine that appeared swollen and looked like a volvulus, or a twisting of the bowel. If that were the case, I should be in a lot of pain, and I wasn't. The doctor suggested I go to prompt care or the ER right away to have this looked at if after one more x-ray the images looked the same. My heart was racing and I knew there was no way I would be able to get to daycare to pick up my son on time. Here I was almost immediately putting my own needs off to avoid...again! I called my husband, and thankfully he was able to support me in this way and pick up our son. God was allowing me the time I needed to get this figured out, but I had to ask for help.

We took the follow-up x-ray and sure enough that area or mass looked the same. I was somewhat in shock. I remembered that sign on the door of the office bathroom, "Things happen for a reason." Had I finally made it to the chiropractor to find this mass or bowel issue?

As I drove home that night, I just sat in silence wondering what was happening. I prayed to God and told Him I trusted Him and I knew He had a plan for me and I would just wait for His instructions on what to do and how to handle things. I decided to go to the ER that next morning to follow up. Anyone who knows me knows I am a planner and spending the entire night in the ER didn't sound fun. So, I chose to go the next day so I could take my son to daycare and avoid having to interrupt his life ☺. Were my control issues popping up?

When I arrived at the ER, I had to wait a few hours. This gave me just enough time to think I was a big fool for being there amidst people who really needed attention to their health. When I finally saw the doctor, his approach wasn't as friendly as I would have liked, which further exacerbated my concern of looking like a fool. I could tell he did not like the source of my information (chiropractor) as he kept drilling me as to why a chiropractor would be diagnosing me with a bowel issue. I had to finally get assertive and stop his interrogation. I explained that the radiologist had concerns and the chiropractor just relayed that message. I was just following up to be a responsible patient and care for myself. He said, "This is just air in your stomach. I could do a battery of tests on you, but I don't think that is necessary." I just looked at him. He looked back and said, "Well, what did you want?" I really had no words (maybe a few I was thinking). I left and I felt even more foolish than I did to begin with.

Let's pause here for a minute. I now have more experience taking steps of faith and this was one of them when I wasn't as confident. Be warned, when you are obedient, you will meet opposition. You will feel a fool. Others will not understand. Keep trusting, keep praying, keep asking for the Lord to guide your steps. Most importantly, KEEP taking steps!

I didn't feel at peace with this scenario yet. God kept tapping me to get a second opinion. After a couple days, I called my primary care doctor and left a message for the nurse to call me back. When she did, she didn't leave the kindest message which discouraged me. I let a few more days go by and tried again. This time, I reached a nurse I really connected with. She listened to my story and encouraged me to come in. She said they could review my x-rays and give me their opinion.

If anyone is counting, I received two rejections before someone listened. Hang in there! (Since this time, I have learned to withstand many more rejections and plod on. You get good at it!)

Christmas Eve rolled around and I went in to see my primary care doctor. He made me feel at ease for coming in and took my case seriously. He did an exam and didn't really find much. Then he said he wanted me to get a CT scan done of my abdomen. That could rule out inflammatory bowel diseases, cancer, or a hernia, all options he felt were possible. He sent me home with a bottle of vanilla barium shake and away I went. The day after Christmas, I drank my shake, went in for the CT, and waited for the results. The next day, my doctor called and said, "Well, it looks like we are following bread crumbs here. The CT showed signs of inflammation which leads me to think you may have an inflammatory bowel disease like Crohn's. I want you to follow up with a GI doctor."

Wow, Crohn's? This was not on my radar. Sure, I have had some weird bowel issues throughout my adult life, but presently, I wasn't experiencing any of those symptoms to any large degree. I went to my GI appointment and he again confirmed this was his initial theory, Crohn's disease, by the way it presented and with my past symptoms. He described treatment options and the medication options which startled me. I may have an autoimmune disease that would lead me to get on strong medication for the REST of my life!! No way! My husband and I were planning to try for our second child and this was not part of my plan! He said he wanted to do a colonoscopy to make a final diagnosis. "Great," I thought. I had heard about these....

My first witness of a physical miracle

Colonoscopy day drew near. I will spare you the details of my prep. ☺ The procedure was quick and painless and as I came out of anesthesia, the GI doctor stopped in to see me. He said, "Good news is, I don't think you have Crohn's disease." "Okay," I thought. "Did you find anything else in there?" I asked almost jokingly. He said, "Well that is the bad news. I actually found what I think is a pre-malignant polyp in your rectum. If you had waited until 40 or 50, you would have had full blown rectal cancer." WOW! I guess that faint thought was in the back of my head, "What if they find something bad," but then with no other findings but this, I thought, "Divine Intervention." Did God lead me to get that x-ray to raise enough concern to get me here to find this pre-malignant polyp? I didn't think it; I knew it! God gave me instructions and thankfully, this time, I listened. But, how easily I could have ignored the whispers with all of the shouts slowing down the answer that was coming.

The GI doctor wanted to do one more follow-up test to insure nothing was going on in the small intestine where that initial concern began. I had an MRE which came back negative for any findings.

Just as I learned about the God thread that ran through the library book, the Kohl's order and staff that assisted me, the tornado, my friend, and all other aspects of my first story to get clothes to that young boy in need, I realized that this time, the God thread worked through several others for MY need. He worked through my friend, the chiropractor, the radiologist, the ER doctor, my primary care doctor, and the GI doctor, all to do the right things needed to find something deadly growing in my body.

Energy: Not created nor destroyed

Glancing at me, anyone would think I was a healthy young woman; however, pain was buried deep inside me that was starting to show up physically. I believe the pain was calling out to me to start caring for myself in a way that I hadn't. To start living a truth I was not living.

As stress levels build in our lives, physical manifestations of this stress begin to rise in our bodies like a balloon about to pop over the heat of a flame. If we are fortunate, we start to seek answers to solve these issues before they develop into something greater. However, often we start by telling a friend or possibly visiting the doctor in the early stages when what we should be doing is reflecting on the emotional issues in our life we are avoiding.

The first law of thermodynamics, the Law of Conservation of Energy, states that energy can neither be created nor destroyed; energy can only be transferred or changed from one form to another.[1]

So, bad energy can set up camp right in our bodies if we don't convert it to positive energy and use it for good. What that means is we need to address our issues or they will literally be worn with us wherever we go, reminding us they are there!

Traditional Reiki For Our Times[2] states, "To create permanent healing, it is necessary to change the mind. To change the mind, it is necessary to change the heart." The author goes on to cite research in psychoneuroimmunology, the study of how mind and body affect immune system, where this theory is supported.

Bad energy can set up camp right in our bodies if we don't convert it to positive energy and use it for good.

Additional studies cited in her book state that positive emotions have shown a positive effect on the regularity of our heartbeat. Scientists have found that if the heartbeat is regular, "it brings corresponding increases in clarity, buoyancy, intuitive awareness, and peacefulness, as well as improves health and a stronger immune system response."

Louise Hay has several books published regarding mind-body connection, the symbolism of various body conditions, and what emotion they may tie to.

According to *Reiki Energy Medicine, Bringing Healing Touch into Home, Hospital, and Hospice*,[3] "Disease is not separate from the body; it is the body out of balance. Rather than being seen as an invader to be attacked and conquered, disease can be understood as an important messenger carrying the word that homeostasis needs to be restored."

According to Louise Hay[4] and cellular biologist Bruce Lipton[5], physical symptoms are "merely tangible evidence of what is going on in your unconscious mind and how you are really feeling deep inside."

I was unaware of these resources at the time of my pre-malignant polyp finding, but as I reflect back, the truth of it leaves me trembling. Cancer represented "long-standing resentment, deep hurt, deep secrets, or grief eating away at the self." Rectum represented the "dumping point." I had a lot of deep hurts, secrets, and grief I needed to dump and I was becoming aware!

Body talk

I thought much differently about my body after this experience. I respected it more and learned it speaks up when out of balance. God designed us at a cellular level and has the ability to restore us; however, we play a role in that healing.

We must listen.

We must believe.

We must act when prompted.

We must trust.

We must delete the need to understand.

We must be thankful that we are
"fearfully and wonderfully made."

I continued to invest in preventative maintenance on my body:

- Exercise.
- Diet: balanced, but with foods of pleasure too! All foods can fit.
- Chiropractic adjustments to align my body.

- Massage to calm and treat muscles to maintain my alignment.
- Reiki to quiet myself and connect with another soul with intention of my deeper healing.

My body and mind was God's temple *(1 Corinthians 6:19)*. He needed it cleaned up so that I was ready to do as He called me to and live a life of abundance!

A mountain to climb

God doesn't fix our problems overnight. He really doesn't fix them at all; we fix them. He just provides us the tools to repair the areas of our lives that have been broken. Have you ever seen the movie *Evan Almighty*[6]? It is a great movie about the story of Noah's Ark, but with some comedy brought into it in a modern-day setting. Morgan Freeman plays God and a good God he is! One line in that movie captures a great message. As he talks to Evan's (Noah's) wife who has become estranged from her husband, Morgan Freeman begins to speak about God's presence in our lives. He said something along these lines: If you pray for patience, God doesn't give you patience, He gives you an opportunity to BE patient. If you pray for your marriage or family to be closer, God gives you a situation to bring your family closer.

If we begin to look at our pain differently, we can take time to reflect on what the pain is telling us. What changes can be made that will get to the root of the pain not just deal with the symptoms.

When our day gets off track at home, I like to do an instant replay of when the day went wrong. We trace back to what happened through the day to pinpoint where the painful feelings started. We are then able to talk through what happened, why the person who is hurt is feeling the way they are, pray about it, and move forward with more peace.

I once heard a quote, "Impression without Expression leads to Depression."

Whether we are impressed upon in a good way or a negative way, if we don't find a healthy way to express it, we may have a negative energy settle in. Expression can be tears, laughter, words, art, movement, singing. Whatever the Lord has blessed you with to express yourself, use it to feel what you need to feel. Don't keep it buried inside.

Being your truest you is a beautiful thing and your body will shine brightly when you do it!

Today, I surrender:
my body.

Lord, show me
the next step
I must take.

Chapter 6
Goals & Discussion

What physical signs in your body are reflective of sins you need to address?

*"I am bent over and racked with pain.
All day long I walk around filled with grief."* ~PSALM 38:6

Our story has returned to the "Sin" portion of our cycle. How has sin affected your body? What physical symptoms have manifested in your body as a result of sin?

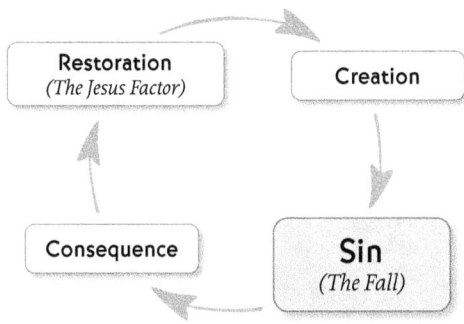

Action Step

Questions to ponder:

1. What experiences in your life have increased the pressure to make a change in your life?

    a. How did you respond to that experience?

b. Did your response to that experience improve or make the situation less favorable?

   c. Reflecting on the response you took, are there any further steps that you could have taken or could still take to achieve a better result?

2. What circumstances or experiences in your life are calling you to address right now?

   a. What can you do right now to take one step forward in addressing your situation(s)?

3. What positive aspect can you find in the difficult circumstances you are going through or already went through?

4. Have you experienced physical or mental conditions that could reflect negative energy that has been stored rather than expressed and released from your body?

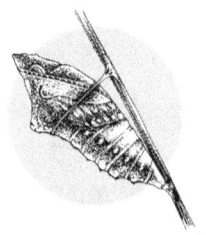

Chapter 7

The Mud and the Mire

"He lifted me out of the pit of despair, out of the mud and the mire."
~PSALM 40:2 (NLT)

Nerves welled up inside me as I got my 2-year-old ready to go. We took a walk to church so I could break my silence on the lie I was living.

What is mire? "A stretch of swampy or boggy ground; a situation or state of difficulty, distress, or embarrassment from which it is hard to extricate oneself."[1]

At 32 years old, I found myself deep in the mud and mire. I was working full time, had a 2-year-old, was trying to conceive a second child, and a marriage that was far from healthy. I found myself so conflicted about trying to conceive a second child that I was overcome with emotion and the Spirit was compelling me to talk about it. I reached out to my Pastor's wife and asked if she would meet with me to talk about a few things. She agreed. I had just gotten to know her in passing at church, but she was such a warm, friendly woman, my first female Christian role model in a leadership role. She and I set a time to meet at the church one weekend morning.

Just to add insult to injury, I was dealing with a major sinus infection, the worst I have ever had. (Recalling mind-body connection, sinus problems relate back to irritation with someone close). I showed up looking quite pathetic to purge the fact that I was in an unhealthy marriage, with a child, and I had been trying to conceive a second child, blowing my nose, sneezing, the works. Did I also mention I was attending a Mennonite church at the time in a small congregation of 40 to 60 on any given Sunday with seemingly nuclear families that fit the mold? In my mind, I was the only person having these problems and I had feared breaking my silence and looking like a fake or a major sinner!

Here goes...I took a deep breath and spilled my story. I could barely make eye contact as I sobbed over the fact that as I was growing in my faith, the gap between my husband and I widened more and more every day. We had become the contradiction of one another in every thought and decision we were making. I was committed to my marriage. I meant my vows. I had highlighted and read and re-read this verse in the Bible:

> "And if a woman has a husband who is not a believer and he is willing to live with her, she must not divorce him. For the unbelieving husband has been sanctified through his wife. Otherwise your children would be unclean, but as it is, they are holy."
>
> ~1 CORINTHIANS 7:12-14

Am I meant to live like this forever?

Do I wait until things are perfect to try for another child?

Do we just move forward and let things settle?

Do we get divorced?

As the weight on my chest lightened, my Pastor's wife shared a story with me. She met me where I was and did not make me feel less than. What happened next was one of the most life-changing things that has ever happened to me. She prayed out loud with me, for me. She grabbed my hand and asked Jesus to help me. Her words were so sincere and genuine. I could feel the Holy Spirit in that room wrapping around me to say, "You are going to be okay." I had taken the first step, by admitting I had a problem! The courage she had to pray with me and the tenderness with which she prayed changed me.

Punch to the gut

Well, I got pregnant and not surprisingly, my problems didn't fade away. In fact, they intensified.

Imagine this: pregnant, sitting in a counselor's office talking about my failing marriage. EMBARRASSING! I felt so dysfunctional and pathetic. Inside I felt like I was on the right path with God, but outside to the world, I felt like a fool. What did I look like?

I began to seek out an additional source of help, a Christian counselor. As I was developing a friendship with my pastor's wife, I was trying another avenue as well as an outlet to get these problems aired and dealt with. The counselor sat and listened to my concerns. She validated them all. She thought I was appropriate in the issues that I brought forward. She suggested a couple of books, which I read and appreciated.

NOT SOLVING MY PROBLEM!

One day at counseling she posed this question, "Julie, do you think it is your job to save your husband?"

Let's sit with this for a minute.

Have you ever had that punch to the gut question?
The one that holds you accountable to your current situation?

Can you ask it to yourself right now and answer honestly?

I responded with…"No," but the painful realization was, you guessed it, I **was** owning that responsibility. I had taken on the responsibility of saving my husband, thinking God had put me in his life to bring him to Christ. OUCH! How ignorant I felt. I know I am supposed to witness and not force, but here I was stressing over this responsibility for fear of the impact on my children if I didn't. That punch to the gut hung with me the entire way home and then some. I still remember that day because it was a big step toward saving my life, my children's lives, and my husband's life.

I didn't like it. I didn't really like her for saying it. I didn't like how I felt about it. But if anything was going to change, I needed to hear those words!

Starting to let go

I started that day to let go of this responsibility I had assigned myself and vowed that I would from that day forward witness and offer grace alone. It was a big step in surrender for me, to begin to stop fighting the issues in my life and begin only reflecting Christ in my actions rather than talking the talk and not walking the walk as genuinely as I should be. It doesn't matter how "right" we are and how "wrong" someone else is. We have to keep shining the light so there is no doubt that Christ lives in us.

> *It doesn't matter how "right" we are and how "wrong" someone else is. We have to keep shining the light so there is no doubt that Christ lives in us.*

When I handed the responsibility of God's will for my husband back to the owner, God, my life didn't get easier, but it got much clearer. I was able to focus on my actions and not my husband's. I began being proud of who I was and what I was doing. I was aligning with God's will, and his plan is always WAY better than mine. I was being a better example for my son. I was reading scripture and feeling tearful as I was listening and doing what it told me. I was "waiting on God's instructions," and doing what He was telling me! Victory!!!

Were all of my problems solved? No. Was I at peace? I was getting there because I knew what I needed to do. I was responsible for me, and God was clearly spelling out my role and actions. The inner peace that followed allowed me to step toward the best me I had been in a long time. As God was pulling me out of the mud and the mire, my mind was clearing up. My outlook was looking up. My heart was healing. My hope was being restored to something greater: God's will for my life and what He could do with me as a faithful servant if I would allow Him to.

I was no longer lost and wandering; I was found and following Jesus.

Pregnant and feeling alone

My pregnancy was overall very healthy, but I had more body ailments this time around. Something unique I developed was Thrombophlebitis, a condition where veins get inflamed. It was painful! I had to begin wearing compression stockings. For those of you who don't know what those are, they are super constricting tights that help your blood to be pumped more efficiently and not pool into your lower extremities. They were a life saver, but it was quite a difficult process to pull those things on.

Picture this:

Rubber gloves on, as if preparing to wash dishes!

Huge belly.

Winter white body.

Can't bend over.

Now prepare for the fight of your life gripping these things and pulling them up with full force. I was quite a pretty picture. ☺ I was a mix between a senior citizen (no offense seniors!), a pregnant woman, and a Hooter's girl. One night I even said, wow, I feel like a Hooter's girl, look at my tan legs. Then, I realized anyone hearing that statement followed by seeing me would say, "NO WAY!" It was a humbling time.

I felt very alone in this pregnancy.

Baby names

As Thanksgiving rolled around, it was time to think about this baby's name. We were waiting to be surprised on the gender. I brainstormed on names and really wanted a significant name related to something spiritual. God pointed me to the story of Hannah.

> *"I prayed for this child, and the Lord has granted me what I asked of him. So now I give him to the Lord. For his whole life he will be given over to the Lord."* ~1 SAMUEL 1:27-28

I immediately felt the Spirit tell me this was a baby boy and he must be named Samuel. This baby growing inside of me was prayed over and sought after. Conceiving this child took many months longer than my first pregnancy with Rylie. I had much more time to think and contemplate this pregnancy and promised God that if I were to get pregnant, I would do all in my power to raise him to follow God's teachings and dedicate his life to serving the Lord.

Those next few weeks and months passed SLOWLY! For any woman reading this who has been pregnant, you know the last month is like the first 8 months combined! I was devastated when I learned my OB was using my ultrasound due date estimate and I was still using my date of last menstrual period. The reality was that it was only one week, count it, one week different, yet I cried in the car when I realized I had another week to go. That little stinker waited right until the end to initiate labor. He was so gentle with me though. I had slow and steady contractions for the entire Sunday. I really wanted to get Rylie to bed before I left for the night. I believe the Lord had His hand in things, since just as I tucked Rylie in bed (after completing books and breathing through painful contractions!), labor intensified quickly. Our babysitter arrived and a few hours later....

That baby growing inside of me was a little boy and he was named Samuel.

I cuddled my newborn little Sam with a feeling much more relaxed than I had the first time. After all, I knew how to change a diaper, I knew how to breastfeed, I knew I would heal. This time, I could just love on this new baby and enjoy his adorable cuteness! One difference this time though, I already had a baby I loved with all my heart. "How will I love them both as much as they need?" I needed to make sure Rylie was okay. My nurse lovingly reminded me that Sam needed me right now and Rylie was fine.

A lesson that I may only have embraced if forced: Letting Go.

I was learning my first big lesson from God that began a transformative process in me. One that catapulted me down the "path to surrender." One that I believe was a reason God gave me this beautiful gift of a second pregnancy amidst my fear and angst over whether it was the right thing to do. A lesson that I may only have embraced if forced: **Letting Go.**

Today, I surrender:
my pain.

*Lord, show me
the next step
I must take.*

Chapter 7
Goals & Discussion

What pain or sin do you need to mentally release for full healing?

"He lifted me out of the pit of despair, out of the mud and the mire." ~PSALM 40:2

Our story has returned to the "Consequence" portion of our cycle. How has sin affected your mind? What mental hang-ups or lies has the enemy been playing in your head as a result of sin?

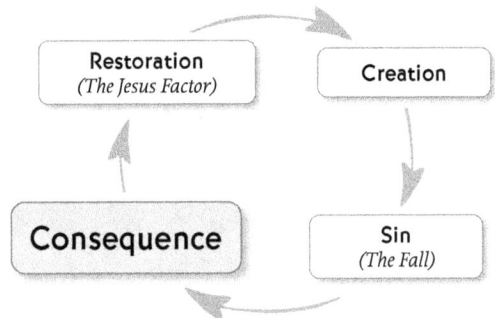

Action Step

Questions to ponder:

1. What mud and mire do you have or have you had in your life?

2. Have you told anyone about it? If not, why?

3. Who could you tell about your mud and mire so that it may help you or another?

4. Have you seen God working in the mud and the mire? Have you thanked Him for it?

5. Have you reflected on what you have learned or could have learned in the mud? *("There is the mud, and there is the lotus that grows out of the mud. We need the mud in order to make the lotus." Thich Nhat Hanh)*

6. Are you still in the mud and mire, and unsure how to get out?

    a. If so, what step could you take right now to begin climbing out?

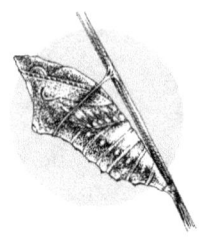

Chapter 8

Sam
"And God taught me to let it go"

"Forget the former things; do not dwell on the past. See, I am doing a new thing! Now it springs up; do you not perceive it? I was making a way in the wilderness and streams in the wasteland."
~ISAIAH 43:18-19

A new baby is like a glimpse of Heaven. In what feels like an eternity, nine months is only a blink in time. That nine months is much like a metaphor for what our life is like waiting to meet with our Father in Heaven. It can feel like an eternity at times, but in reality will be just a blink and then bliss.

"For God so loved the world, that He gave His only Son, that whoever believes in Him shall not perish, but have eternal life." ~JOHN 3:16

Becoming a mom made this verse very significant. Experiencing the gift of a baby helped me to better understand the sacrifice God made by sending something vulnerable that He loved with all His heart into a sinful world where He would be unappreciated, tortured, and killed.

Imagine taking your brand new baby, that God gave to you (don't forget), and dropping it off in a place you don't feel safe and hoping for the best. Let's add on that God came down and told you, "Trust me, this child will grow up and transform the hearts of everyone in this place. Just let go." Could you do it then? For my animal lovers out there, think about your new puppy. Could you take that sweet little puppy and drop it off in a dog park full of large, unfamiliar dogs that were all fending for themselves?

It is hard to imagine, but He did it! I never could fully empathize with this or "get it." Having children allowed me to really admire and respect our Father. It made me love Him. We are supposed to love Him and would say we do if we are believers, but do you? It is hard to love someone when we don't see them or understand them from our human perspective. That is the beauty of Jesus. He knew we needed that human connection to better understand Him. He wanted to relate to us.

Think back to that child or pet you adore. Do you spend hours, days, weeks, months, and years learning their ins and outs so you can understand how to make them laugh or smile? What will comfort them? What makes them sad or angry? What will cheer them up when they are down or lonely? How to provide a pep talk when they need it? That is how well God knows each of us. He is waiting on us to believe that and then start talking to Him about our thoughts, big and small, so that He can give us the keys to unlock ourselves and enter the door to our best life. This awesome personal relationship requires something though—SURRENDER— followed by patience and listening. It isn't a one and done thing. It is a constant check-in process so

He can guide each step. He won't steal your attention from the world, but He will patiently wait until you figure out you need Him. When you do, His love will pour out and fill you so full that you will spill it out to others and continue the growth of His kingdom here on Earth.

All of a sudden you are filled with gratitude. *Thank you, Father, for trusting me so much that You sent one of Your souls to dwell in this home so that I may tend to and care for it in such a way that is pleasing to You. You had faith in me, and I won't let you down! I will tend to this little lamb as well as I can to keep him in your flock.*

Breastfeeding and a two-year-old!

The second child ventures out a lot more than the first! I took Sam by a cupcake shop on the way home from the hospital. Yes, I was wearing pajamas, those beautiful post-partum underpants with the largest pad you have ever seen. I had labored out a child, likely slept less than an hour, and didn't care what I looked like in public or what germs my child was exposed to (This was pre-COVID ☺). Ahhh, the freedom of "been there, done that!" Contrast this to when Rylie was born. I didn't leave the house for six weeks, which is what the doctor had instructed. In fact, my visit to the OB was my first time out after his birth, and I felt like I had been under a rock! I am not sure I had even brushed my teeth on a regular basis. I felt like an alien visiting an unfamiliar planet.

I knew having a second child would add a new element of complexity to my life, but you really can't prepare yourself exactly for how things will go. You just have to dive in. After a couple of weeks being home, I got adventurous and decided we could take the two of them to a gymnastics free-play time. It would be fun for Rylie, and I could just pack Sam in this ring sling I had purchased, which was AMAZING! Besides looking like a shepherd woman from Jesus' time, I had some freedom and didn't even care!

Immediately after arriving, Sam needed to breastfeed. This was a little disappointing to me. I was really hoping to follow around after Rylie and enjoy his experience. Instead, I had to sit on the outskirts feeding Sam while his dad did the fun stuff. I felt a pang of anxiety, fear, and disappointment creep up. Then the voice of God gently blew by saying, "Your role is to be present with Sam right now; let that go." I took a breath and did my best to enjoy that moment with Sam. Rylie was fine after all and who else could breastfeed my child? That was really a privilege and a gift; why was I taking it for granted?

CONTROL! I wasn't in control. I was being forced to do something I didn't want to do when I didn't want to do it, and I didn't like it. It made me feel uncomfortable, left out, disappointed, and like a big baby myself. Sigh. An old pattern was creeping up again.

The story doesn't end there...God gave me many more opportunities to practice letting go, such as when I was at a store and had a child in a stroller and a little hand in my open hand and couldn't get a door. When I had two children needing my immediate attention for differing needs. When I had one child needing a diaper change and another vomiting in the bathroom. When I had one child climbing in my bed and another crying for a feeding or a diaper change. The list goes on and on. God was doing something here. I had prayed for this child and put much thought into it. He may have taken a big pause while this plan came into action, but when the trigger was pulled, the gift had a much bigger purpose than a cute baby to cuddle and a growing family to experience life with. One piece of that purpose was my surrender. I no longer had a choice to live with the illusion that I was in control. It was very evident EVERY moment, every hour, and every day of my life.

> *I no longer had a choice to live with the illusion that I was in control.*

Yikes! What does life look like when you surrender control? I hadn't experienced it before. Either I would break, screw up my children, or run myself into the ground; I had no other choice, but to look up.

Being a single parent while married

About this time, my husband was entering a busy season in his career. He was coming off of a several-month layoff and starting to work many hours. When I headed back to work, I frankly was living the life of a single parent. I had primary responsibility for drop off, pick up, and surviving the night. Not to mention getting the kids ready in the morning and, oh yeah, working a full time job. Two nights a week, my husband was in class until after the children's bedtime. Sadly, we were not sharing the role of parenting and managing daily life. Eventually, I got pretty adventurous. I thank Rylie for that. I didn't want a second child to stop us from experiencing life together. He was coming into an age where everything was new and exciting and different, and I enjoyed doing new things with him. So, I started to step out of my comfort zone and figure out how to do life with an infant and a three-year-old. We were quite the team (still are). I was proud of the things we would accomplish together. We enjoyed trips to the grocery store, park, the cupcake shop (yes, we love this place!), even the children's museum. Did I mention church? Yes, I managed an infant and a three-year-old at church by myself. It was painful at times, and many times we missed most of the service being in the bathroom, but we did it!

The patience I saw in Rylie was amazing. He would wait while I managed chaos. He would wait while I changed diapers. He would listen to crying without flinching. He would wait to have me play tag until I had Sam secure. He modeled so much patience. God had provided him opportunities to develop his character through our dynamic—how cool is that?

Letting go was liberating! I was doing things I didn't think possible because I was letting God lead the experiences. I was expecting chaos and He was offering solutions along the way. He would provide a patient child, a friendly passerby who could provide us aid, and perseverance inside me to keep going. This letting go didn't stop at home. I took it back to work with me. Before my maternity leave, I was looking at another job. I didn't think I could manage the stress any longer. I didn't get the new job and I accepted that as I trusted God's plan. So He revealed to me while I was on leave that He wanted me right where I was, but I needed to make an adjustment. I needed to surrender my role to Him so He could help me do it better. So I did.

> *God breathed new life into my professional world and helped me manage the chaos in my life. It felt good. I felt alive. I had purpose. I had vision.*

I began to delegate more. I was more assertive in my conversations and business dealings. I had doors opened to provide student relationships which would enable me to get projects done not otherwise possible on my own. I had shifted employees into positions they thrived in to better support our department. I had a renewed appreciation for my job and enjoyment of it. God breathed new life into my professional world and helped me manage the chaos in my life that no longer felt like chaos. It felt good. I felt alive. I had purpose. I had vision. God had a role for me, and I wanted to fill it to the best of my ability.

Letting go in marriage

Slowly, I had been allowing God to take the lead in my parenting, my profession, my friendships, my finances, and other areas of my personal growth. Letting go was feeling great, but my body began reminding me I was still holding something—something big.

If I had only known now that my body was trying to communicate with me to help me. It was screaming at me!

- During pregnancy with Sam, varicose veins;
- Shortly after Sam's birth, strep throat times 2;
- Months later, an unknown cause (allergic reaction?) which caused my tongue to swell;
- Continued nagging pain in my right upper back/shoulder area;
- Toenails took a beating during pregnancy and I had to visit a podiatrist.

LORD, help! I am letting go. I am letting You lead. Come on now, help a daughter out.

But God hadn't forgotten me. He saw me. He saw my pain. He cared for my body. Remember how we can keep pushing down a sin, that choice that separated us from God's will, and we keep going. Yep... eating away at my body. The something BIG I still had to deal with that was in need of new management: my marriage. We still needed a rescue of Epic Proportions.

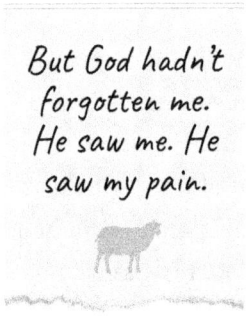
But God hadn't forgotten me. He saw me. He saw my pain.

In Chapter 6, I mention the mind-body connection. Louise Hay has put much research into study on what various areas of the body represent and the mental connection "theme" it ties back to. You may be a skeptic of that. I had never thought about this until I heard of it and began looking up the meaning of my various body ailments and BAM! I was literally walking in my pain every day. The areas in which I was physically hurting represented the exact things I was thinking, feeling, and needing to take action on.

Those compression stockings were helping me manage varicose veins. Varicose veins represent "standing in a situation you hate. Discouragement, and feeling overworked and overburdened."[1] BAM!

Toenails…toes represent "the minor details of the future." BAM!

Strep throat—times 2. Since it had been such a short time since the previous time I had it, they discussed removing my tonsils as an adult! Infection: "irritation, anger, annoyance." Throat: "the inability to speak up for oneself, swallowed anger, stifled creativity, and refusal to change." The odd tongue swelling—tongue: "represents the ability to taste the pleasures of life with joy." BAM!

Yep, my body was angry with me. It was hurting. My mouth took the toughest beating, and it was telling me it was time to SPEAK! Not to just speak, but to

Speak TRUTH!

A truth I was avoiding because I feared the consequences of doing so, which was the fear of chaos in my home. Most discussions went something like this:

- Build courage to speak.
- Find best way to bring up topic.
- Quickly silenced with "Shut up, you are the problem if you are bringing it up; you will never be happy."
- Despair.
- Put on a happy face to pull through the night with kids.
- Silence and avoidance with partner.

After years of this, it was easier to work on ME than US. It was clear that this pattern could no longer continue, but HOW God? The rescue we needed was so far beyond my expertise. It got worse before it got better, but God was able to use my surrender to chase the enemy out of my family. He now had at least one of us tuned in and aware of Satan's schemes and I was ready to obey!

An encounter with the enemy vs the Holy Spirit

The difficulty in my marriage was reaching a climax. One weekend morning, he left for town. Upon his return, he and I began to have a disagreement. To be honest, I don't recall what started it. I hesitated to argue as I didn't want my home to be a war zone for my children. I just wanted a good day. I asked gently that he stop yelling, and he continued to follow me around the house trapping us in various rooms to fight with me. The kids and I were trying to get to the park. So I kept doing my best to get us ready and out the door. He finally blocked the doorway to Rylie's room where we all were. He didn't censor his language, which is one reason I didn't like engaging with him. It was never a fair fight or discussion. I refused to have this argument that would not have a positive conclusion, and sent my kids under his leg out the bedroom door. He allowed that. I then started to crawl and he pressed his knee so hard into my back that I got scared and it hurt. At that moment, I felt what I am certain now was the Holy Spirit rise within me and lift me out of that room, to the other side. I felt like I grew a foot taller and floated down the hallway. I remained calm and scooted out of the house with my children, packing the stroller and walking down the sidewalk as fast as I could. It was almost as if angels came under each of my arms and carried me away. Something had to change…I was getting closer.

The time was nearing for me to SPEAK.

Groceries

Tension continued to build. Soon after, I was given another opportunity for action. One of the main duties I could count on my husband to do was pick up groceries. I would make the list, organize it by section, and he would do the grocery shopping. I tremendously appreciated it. Well, with him around less because of work and other plans, there were several home projects barely started or half-way to completion, and fall was approaching. I learned of a new service that a local grocery store was providing (we likely ALL use it now!), grocery pick up! I thought this was a great idea that would save him a couple hours and we could knock out some projects. I started to get the list together and asked him what hour window that Saturday he was willing and able to go pick up the pre-ordered groceries. He started to argue with me. He did not want to do this. He did not want to commit to a time, and it inconvenienced his day. I didn't fully understand why this was becoming a problem, but it was quickly escalating beyond control. His anger built up to a point of him calling me a "F*****g b***h" while I held my one-year-old and my three-year-old was in bed attempting to take a nap, which never truly began. You can only imagine my horror as those evil words came from his mouth upon the ears of my precious children who I was doing my best to raise to follow Jesus. It was as if God grabbed my shoulders and shook me like a ragdoll. He screamed, "You need to do more than just pray, daughter." Time to take action! I gathered my children quickly to go get those groceries, and as I walked out the door, I looked him in the eye and said, "You won't bring me down."

I SPOKE! Truth.

I battled with Satan that day. Instead of silencing his voice, my husband was speaking his voice. My new armor was allowing me to see that my husband was prisoner to the enemy's schemes. I wasn't falling for it this time.

I sent a text to one of my trusted friends of the faith and told her to pray, and pray hard. That night I lay awake while my house was asleep. I walked into my living room and was shaking, trembling, scared. I began to cry out to God. I beat my hands with a fist begging God to make clear my next steps. I pleaded that I believed He wanted me out, but I wanted to know for sure it was coming from His instruction. I wrestled with the Lord and He won. This truly was the night I made a complete surrender and said, "Let Your will be done. Save me. Save my children. Save my husband. Save us. I am scared and I don't know how to do this."

My knighting ceremony

> *"Finally, be strong in the Lord and in his mighty power. Put on the full armor of God so that you can take your stand against the devil's schemes. For our struggle is not against flesh and blood, but against the rulers, against the authorities, against the powers of this dark world and against the spiritual forces of evil in the heavenly realms. Therefore put on the full armor of God, so that when the day of evil comes, you may be able to stand your ground, and after you have done everything, to stand."* ~EPHESIANS 6:10-13

I was a soldier about to head into battle, a battle against forces beyond my ability to fight alone. The battle was not against my husband, but against the schemes of the devil who had taken over my home. We were all victims to his lies, and the Lord was lighting my way to save our entire family. The night I surrendered, our Father "knighted" me in preparation for the difficulties that would lie ahead. As I knelt before Him, it was as if He said these words:

> *"Stand firm then with the belt of truth buckled around your waist, with the breastplate of righteousness in place,"* ~EPHESIANS 6:14

He was telling me to be in my Bible daily, hearing His voice through scripture so that I was filled with truth at all times. It was important that I remembered I was worthy and chosen and my heart must be protected.

> *"and with your feet fitted with the readiness that comes from the gospel of peace."* ~EPHESIANS 6:15

He would be calling me to action. I would need to be a doer of the Word, not just a hearer. I would be fighting this battle with peace, His way.

> *"In addition to all this, take up the shield of faith, with which you can extinguish all the flaming arrows of the evil one."* ~EPHESIANS 6:16

Arrows were heading my direction, arrows that could take me down if I did not have faith that God was truly leading me to safety. Lies were coming and my faith must stay intact.

> *"Take the helmet of salvation and the sword of the Spirit, which is the word of God."* ~EPHESIANS 6:17

I must not forget that my surrender was saving me. That my weapon was God's Word upon my lips directed through the Holy Spirit.

> *"And pray in the Spirit on all occasions with all kinds of prayers and requests. With this in mind, be alert and always keep on praying for all the Lord's people. Pray also for me, that whenever I speak, words may be given me so that I will fearlessly make known the mystery of the gospel, for which I am an ambassador in chains. Pray that I may declare it fearlessly, as I should."* ~EPHESIANS 6:18-20

I was to pray constantly for wisdom and guidance. My words were of utmost importance at this time. I would be tempted more than ever to react with words that would not reflect the Lord, and I must be careful. I had to be brave.

Until this moment, the devil had me locked in chains. I was up against the wall with chains around my arms, legs, and neck. My voice was weak. My hope was bleak. My light was almost out. If He hadn't trusted me with those two sweet souls, Rylie and Sam, I may have stayed chained there forever serving the wrong master. But God fought for me. He woke me up and said, "It is time to stand up and fight, daughter. I have your back, let's do this!"

The night I surrendered, I served a new master. I became an ambassador in chains to the one true God that would set me free. Set my children free. Set my husband free. I believe He will reach through right now and set you free from whatever chains are holding you back.

He taught me that surrender and submission doesn't mean being quiet and doing whatever the loudest voice in your life tells you. It isn't about keeping peace. It is about *making* peace.

> *"...the righteous are as bold as a lion."* ~PROVERBS 28:1

It was time to be a lion, to stand up for what was right, in the right way, and to make long lasting peace, not just peace for a night.

> *"Make every effort to live in peace with everyone and to be holy; without holiness no one will see the Lord."* ~HEBREWS 12:14

You can't make peace if you aren't willing to take a stand for it.

God gained a new soldier that night. He awakened me, He called me, He prepared me, and it was my time to take action.

Deliverance

I had begged the Lord for deliverance from my pain for years. I had many ways I thought it could happen and I offered Him my ideas. I am sure He appreciated them (☺). When it came down to my deliverance, it took something much different than my ideas. Instead of problem gone, poof, it went more like:

1. Acknowledge problem
2. Seek help for problem
3. Pray, pray, pray
4. Surrender
5. Prepare
6. Step of faith (take action!)

Being saved takes knowing you need to be saved, saying you need to be saved, and believing you can be saved. If you don't believe it, you won't ask for, listen to, or follow God's instructions. He can't lead you out of your situation if you won't listen to Him. You won't listen to Him if you didn't ask because you aren't waiting on His words.

God asks us to do hard things. He didn't swoop up Moses and the Israelites and fly them across the Red Sea or have a boat docked for them to climb on. No, He:

1. Talked to Moses about the problem.
2. Told Moses He needed his help.
3. Moses prayed.
4. Moses surrendered and followed God's order.
5. God prepared him with the right people and words.

Moses had to have faith to speak the words and return time after time to Pharaoh.

To top that, even after following those steps, Moses had to repeat these steps each time he made a step of faith, including an apparent deliverance to be met by the Red Sea in which he had to again have faith to place that staff in the sea and trust God to part it.

God will deliver us, but it takes some hard work on our part. Freedom isn't free, but it is worth every ounce of effort.

Psalm 40 refers to God pulling us out of the "mud and the mire." Sometimes we are in the mud and mire and we don't even realize it. It is all we know. Often we have to get out of the mud and mire to realize how deep in it we were.

Only after our surrender can He place us on the Rock.

My deliverance took time. It wasn't the next day after I spoke. The Lord was patient with me and the years it took me to find HIM,

My deliverance took time.

surrender to HIM, and speak HIS truth. He was also patient with my husband. Despite the fact that He had won me back, He had a son He wanted back too, and He needed me to hang in there and fight alongside Him through my obedience.

Third Shift

A lot had transpired those last weeks and months. I had surrendered. I had my armor on. I had spoken truth. What now?

Well, an interesting thing occurred. My husband got switched to third shift. So for the next couple weeks we had a trial "separation," a timeout. We got to experience life apart and conversation quieted. I knew the battle was not over, it was preparation time for what was to come. I was scared.

The day came when third shift was over. Life was going to return to normal—were we ready? We planned to meet that Saturday in town at a festival for lunch. I had the kids ready and he never came. I finally received a text that work ran late and he would meet us at home.

I came home to lay the kids down for a nap. I put a new game I had purchased on the table to play later that night as a family, and began to mop the kitchen. When my husband arrived home, he was in exercise clothes. The pain of realizing he chose the gym over us hurt. As he leaned against the counter, I started to tell about some of the tough parenting moments I had that day. He followed the conversation with, "Well, I am heading to a party at my co-worker's house tonight." The same co-worker he had been working the last two weeks on third shift with.

Pain. Hurt. Disappointment.

He hadn't seen his family in a couple weeks. The kids were napping, so he still hadn't seen them, and he was leaving again.

The peace that transcends all human understanding came over me as the Spirit led me to say the words that delivered my family from the enemy's control.

"To say that our marriage is on the rocks is an understatement. You haven't seen us in weeks, you did not come today, and you plan to leave again tonight. Do we need to separate to get some clarity?"

Nothing fancy, just words of truth. The reply came as quickly as my statement was complete.

"Yes, I think we do."

Relief!

Disbelief.

Fear.

Hurt.

Truth.

He packed a bag, took a shower, got dressed, and left. By now the kids had awakened and as we sat in the treehouse out back, we heard the truck rumble away. No goodbye. The boys had no understanding of what had just happened, but I did.

The Lord had followed through on His promise. And though we would "walk through the valley of the shadow of death, we would fear no evil for His rod and His staff would comfort us" in the days, weeks, months, and years to come.

Thank you, Father.

Today, I surrender:
<u>my voice</u>.

Lord, show me
the next step
I must take.

Chapter 8
Goals & Discussion

Has God created a way to relieve you, deliver you, or open a door for you to freedom?

> *"Forget the former things; do not dwell on the past.*
> *See, I am doing a new thing! Now it springs up; do you not*
> *perceive it? I was making a way in the wilderness and*
> *streams in the wasteland."* ~ISAIAH 43:18-19

Our story has returned to the "Restoration" or "Jesus Factor" portion of our cycle. After acknowledging your sins and addressing their consequences in your life, can you observe how restoration has started to take place?

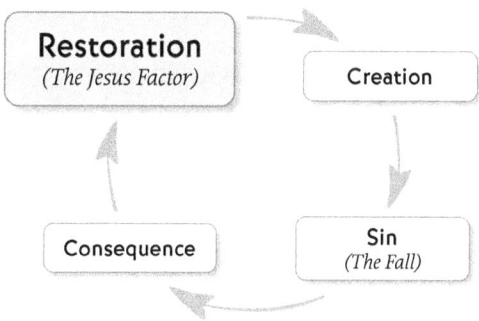

Action Step

Questions to ponder:

1. What situations or circumstances in your life are begging you to let go of control?

2. Are there situations or circumstances in your life that you have already let go of control?

    a. What were they?

    b. What steps did you have to take to let go?

3. If you are having difficulty letting go of control in a particular set of circumstances or several, what is holding you back?

    a. Fear? Be honest, fear of what? Say it out loud or write it down. Tell God about it!

    b. What good could come from letting go?

    c. What bad would come from letting go?

4. Can you identify any truths that you believe should be voiced and acted on? If so, what are they?

   a. Have you asked God for help on these areas of concern?

Part 3
The Butterfly

The butterfly lives in full color. It has the privilege to fly wherever it pleases across beautiful landscape to rest upon colorful flowers. However, before it can fly, did you know a butterfly needs the light from the sun to warm its muscles in order to take off in flight? Just like us, even once we transform closer into God's vision of our true selves, we need His light to fully release and take off to live out our true mission.

When butterflies are in a group, they are called a kaleidoscope. A kaleidoscope is an instrument that you look through in which patterns are seen based on reflections made in mirrors. What we see is a beautiful array of colors. When we, butterflies, take to the sky we form a kaleidoscope, a beautiful, colorful reflection of God's image.

Chapter 9
Becoming a Butterfly

> *"I waited patiently for the Lord; he turned to me and heard my cry. He lifted me out of the slimy pit, out of the mud and mire; he set my feet on a rock and gave me a firm place to stand. He put a new song in my mouth, a hymn of praise to our God. Many will see and fear the Lord and put their trust in Him. Blessed is the one who trusts in the Lord, who does not look to the proud, to those who turn aside to false gods.* ~PSALM 40:1-4

After 12 years, I lost the battle of "saving" my husband, but I gained the victory of knowing God would step in and fill that role much more effectively than I had. He hadn't asked me to do that after all; I had taken that assignment on my own will. Now I was free to live as my best self, using my spiritual gifts to glorify God in a way that brought me peace and joy, the way He intended my life, ALL of our lives, to be. If we invite the Spirit to dwell in us, fruits of the Spirit will abound.

> *"But the fruit of the Spirit is love, joy, peace, patience, kindness, goodness, faithfulness, gentleness, and self-control. Against such things there is no law."* ~GALATIANS 5:22-23

The Bible does not instruct us to endure misery or long-suffering if not in keeping with its teaching. We get no extra points for sticking out unnecessarily painful situations if we are not serving God in them any longer.

He does not expect us to fight battles that are out of our league to fight. We are to stand firm in His Word and allow Him to do the most difficult work.

> *"For the Lord your God is he who goes with you to fight for you against your enemies, to give you the victory."* ~DEUTERONOMY 20:4 (ESV)

We must not be a barrier to His mission of saving lives. When we attempt to act as a "savior" to others, we are only holding ourselves and others back from God's intended outcome.

We need consequences. Sometimes, we need to sit in the silence and loneliness of our truth for God to work on us. The saying "misery loves company" proves true many times. We must not find ourselves in company with the enemy, but instead seek only our Father in Heaven who will keep our paths straight.

As a caterpillar, I was crawling in my faith and relationship with Jesus. I was aware of it. I realized the importance of it, but I was still living in fear and believing I had some control. I was vulnerable to the dangers of the world, and dependent on the circumstances around me and the resources under my feet.

As my chrysalis formed, I was heading away from the mud and seeing clearly that I needed protection and help. I was reaching out to our Father for guidance and protection. He was wrapping me up in a chrysalis of shelter through the mire I was working through.

> *"For I know the plans I have for you, declares the Lord, plans to prosper you and not to harm you, plans to give you a hope and a future."* ~JEREMIAH 29:11-12

God wrapped His loving arms around me spiritually through the fellowship of wonderful friends and neighbors. He sent His people just when needed to tend to His caterpillar who was slowly becoming the butterfly He designed her to be. For *"God is within her, she will not fall," (Psalm 46:5).* The separation between creator and world was becoming clearer as the chrysalis guarded the influence of the outside world. The caterpillar could focus on what God was designing her to do and become. No distraction or dangers took precedence any longer.

I waited with anticipation to emerge as a "butterfly." What would it look like—what was this magical thing that was going to happen to transform my life? I sat and reflected with God on what I would accomplish next. He was making my life to the outside world match what He was doing on the inside of me. As a family, we re-designed our home, and prayed, "Father, help us fill these walls with your Truth." When we were done, no one could enter our house without knowing where our faith, love, and hope were directed. We are commanded to do this:

Deuteronomy 6:6-9: *"These commandments that I give you today are to be on your hearts. Impress them on your children. Talk about them when you sit at home and when you walk along the road, when you lie down and when you get up. Tie them as symbols on your hands and bind them on your foreheads. Write them on the doorframes of your houses and on your gates."*

I had learned why this was so important. This is a portion of our Armor of God:

> *"Stand firm then, with the belt of truth buckled around your waist,"*
> ~EPHESIANS 6:14

The Armor of God starts with the belt of truth. After reading more about the attire of a Roman soldier, the belt played an important role in holding all key pieces together including the sword and other protective gear. Without it, all pieces could fall off or be ineffective. God's Word is our belt of truth, and without constant reminder, that piece of our armor is at risk of enemy attack. Not only does it strengthen me and guide how I lead my boys, but it has the ability to strengthen anyone who enters my home and is empowered with God's Word. It sends a message, "enemy, get out!"

> *"As for me and my house, WE WILL SERVE THE LORD."*
> ~JOSHUA 24:15 (ESV)

There will be no question who the Lord of our life is, and we aren't afraid to proclaim it verbally, in our actions, or on our walls. When the Spirit truly takes over, you can't get enough of it! You just want more, more, more!

For this next leg of the journey, the Lord led me to a new church home to help me grow in the places I needed to most. The worship music uplifted me in a new way. The association to my children's school grew our fellowship experience. As I sat with my pastor to discuss my testimony, we reflected and spoke about my story. He asked, "Have you ever thought about getting baptized?" I responded with, "Well, I was as a baby in the Catholic church. I didn't know I could again." He responded with, "Absolutely you can get baptized again." As he was speaking, my heart began to race. I felt the Spirit running through me saying, "YES, YES, YES! This is what I have been leading you to. You have seen My ways, you have followed them, and you are living in the light. Proclaim this in front of others so they may believe."

> *"And now what are you waiting for? Get up, be baptized and wash your sins away, calling on his name."* ~ACTS 22:16

The magical butterfly that I was waiting to see appear was happening right within me. I was that butterfly emerging from my chrysalis. Ready to enter the world.

> *"You will not have to fight this battle. Take up your positions; stand firm and see the deliverance the Lord will give you."*
> ~2 CHRONICLES 20:17

I thought my growing was done for a while. I was faithful, I had made it through my divorce, and my children were doing well. "I'm good." I did it again, got comfortable and thought I was okay. Then God reminded me I am never done growing and evolving. He had a special day planned for me to get baptized and shout my story to the world bringing glory to His name for deliverance from my mire.

> *"I waited patiently for the Lord; He turned to me and heard my cry. He lifted me out of the slimy pit, out of the mud and mire; He set my feet on a rock and gave me a firm place to stand. He put a new song in my mouth, a hymn of praise to our God. Many will see and fear the Lord and put their trust in Him. Blessed is the one who trusts in the Lord, who does not look to the proud, to those who turn aside to false gods."* ~PSALM 40:1-4

Our Father said, "Now little one, I heard you cry, I lifted you out of the slimy pit, I put your feet on a rock. You will sing My praise so that others will see Me and trust Me."

Being baptized in my late thirties with my children sitting in the congregation was one of the most significant moments of my life. I am so thankful my pastor took time to ask me that simple question. I am so glad I said yes. I am also grateful that I allowed myself to evolve into a new church family. While loyalty to our church is very important, God's leading in our life geographically can take us to new places which is scary; however, He always has a plan and purpose and we must trust it is for our own growth and for the growth of those around us.

I'm a Christian. I'm all In! Now what?

It is exhilarating to surrender your will to God. It is amazing to be delivered from an extremely painful situation. It is motivating to have complete focus on an all-knowing God, illuminating an ultimate truth. Then, you have to get up and go to work, make dinner, raise your kids, and everything else this life expects of us. When this supernatural experience happens, it can be difficult to know how to move on.

I mentioned earlier that life doesn't get easier because you are a Christian; however, your decisions become much clearer. So, that is where I started, one decision at a time. I asked God to show me what surrender looked like in all aspects of my life. If I were to be a disciple and leave everything behind and follow Him, what would that look like? Well, it didn't take long for God to start showing me how to detach from earthly chains and fully attach to Him.

> *Life doesn't get easier because you are a Christian; however, your decisions become much clearer.*

Step one: Give Him my money (pay off financial debts).

Step two: Give Him my relationships (kids, family, other).

Step three: Give Him my goals (personal, professional).

Step four: Become available (sold my home and shed many material possessions to relocate where He called us).

Step five: Walk on water (take big steps of faith).

Step six: Keep walking. Keep trusting.

Step seven: Keep sharing the story.

Step eight: Experience death...

Rolling the stone

"Jesus told them, 'Roll away the stone.' Then Martha said, 'But Lord, it's been four days since he died—by now his body is already decomposing!'" ~JOHN 11:39 (TPT)

Roll the stone. Such a simple command; yet why the hesitation to obey? Did Jesus care about a smell that may waft out from the tomb of Lazarus?

The pastor at my current church did a fantastic sermon series on the seven sign miracles of Jesus told in the book of John. The piece de resistance (aside from the resurrection of Jesus) was raising Lazarus from the dead. I mean wowza! Mark Batterson wrote a great book, *The Grave Robber*,[1] that outlines these miracles in detail. His research into the awe and wonder of God's miracles is a must read.

How does a miracle in Jesus' time apply to you? Well, our pastor laid out this question to us, that I will ask you:

"What is the stone that you need to roll away in your life?"

Jesus didn't just roll away the stone, make it rise, crush it to bits, turn it into birds that flutter away, or some other magical disappearing act. He required an act of obedience and a step of faith on Martha's behalf. Permission to actually do it...and she hesitated...because of a potential smell.

That got me thinking, what stone do I need to roll away? I had a situation in my life that was definitely grieving me, but I had rolled every stone and it wasn't my turn for stone rolling. I told God who I thought needed to roll the stone and it wasn't me. A few days later, when God had me alone, He said, "Yep—it's you, and here is your stone."

Sigh. No thank you. I left a career for You, and gave up a lot of material things for You. I walked through a divorce and stepped away from my family for a few years to grow stronger with You. I will give You my life, but You are asking me to do that?

The stone was a simple question I needed to ask someone. A question that would lead to revealing a painful truth that I wasn't ready to face. A question that would put me in a vulnerable place at risk of being hurt again by disappointment.

Hmmmmm.

I said yes, but asked the Lord to provide me with the exact words because I was terrified.

Stone rolled. Here we go, miracle coming! Come on out, Lazarus!

Empty tomb.

My miracle didn't happen.

This is cruel.

I am not sure I trust You anymore.

Have you been in this place before? You believed you were following the Lord in obedience and got blindsided with a painful blow? Have you ever believed you were doing the right things and they did not end up happily ever after?

We are not alone. Jesus himself felt this way. He was betrayed by Judas, denied by Peter, and finally crucified by the very people He came to give life to. His cry upon the cross shows the grief He experienced when facing death. He felt forgotten by His own Father.

"My God, my God, why have you forsaken me?" ~MATTHEW 27:46

If you are a Marvel fan, you have likely seen *End Game*[2]. The Hulk is on the hunt for the green infinity stone. He meets up with the sorcerer supreme. He approaches to grab the stone, and she puts a hand up and literally knocks his soul from his body. That is about how I felt after my stone was rolled. It took me days, weeks, months, maybe longer to acknowledge the truth that was unfolding in front of me.

A future changed. Past choices now filled with doubt. Faith shaken. I had one last earthly desire that was ripped from me. I felt the accuser laughing at me. I could imagine him saying this:

"You fool. Look how you obediently followed the Lord for years. You believed His promises and now look at you. You have nothing to show for it. I took it from you. Where is your God now?"

Death.

Something died in me that day. A dream, a hope, a wish, a desire, a prayer...hundreds of prayers, left unanswered and unfulfilled. I was left and felt forsaken.

I love to sing, especially praise music at church, but the day I died inside, a song with the line, "I will trust you Jesus" played and I couldn't sing. I couldn't say it, because I wasn't sure anymore. I was masked (thanks to COVID ☺), so no one was aware of my struggle, but God....

> *"I see you," whispered the Lord. In that moment, I realized, He shared my pain.*

Our pastor stopped the song and said, "I sense someone in this room has lost their faith. They aren't sure if they should trust anymore. Let me tell you, keep trusting, don't lose your faith."

"I see you," whispered the Lord. My Father saw me and wrapped His arms around me. He wept too. In that moment, I realized, He shared my pain. He didn't cause it. Sin, sin caused my pain. Circumstances changed, God didn't. My obedience wasn't in vain. God loves us so much He allows free will. He lets us make our own choices so that we can freely choose Him. Even when we choose Him, not everyone in our life will choose Him too. This can leave us in "Havilah," a Hebrew word for "writhing in pain" and "to bring forth." It also means the making of something beautiful through pain.[3]

We sing, "Death, where is your sting?" and reflect on Jesus' death on a cross, but how do we relate to that here, now, in our own life?

Death isn't always a physical death.

Death is the end of something that was significant to us

It can be the loss of innocence through an assault, the physical death of a loved one, a divorce, or loss of a dream. All different losses, yet the pain is the same.

In the days following my "empty tomb" experience, I pondered death and God's goodness. I, who often probably annoy others with my positivity, was getting a glimpse of what it feels like to doubt.

"God must not want this for me." "He tricked me." "Am I being punished for something?" "Did I hear You wrong?!"

No, what was taken from me was a result of His adversary, sin, which robs us of our blessings that He wanted for us too. That "sin" may very well be our own desire that did not align with God's timing.

I kept re-reading the miracle of Lazarus' resurrection. What did I miss? What miracle am I missing? God what, why?

Then, love broke through. I read this description in a Disciple Bible Study workbook under a section titled "Weeping turned to Witness."[4]

"Lazarus came forth covered with grave wrappings. But Jesus left 'the linen wrappings lying there' and the head cloth carefully 'rolled up in a place by itself' *(John 20:6-7)*. The grave cloths indicated that no one had taken Jesus away. Jesus left death behind. Just as no one took His life from Him, so no one took His death from Him; He walked away from it."

He walked away from it. Death.

Death, the something that is significant to us. He didn't just wad up those grave cloths and say "Curse you death." He nicely folded them up, respectfully laid them down, and walked (not ran) away.

God enabled me to respond to my situation as Jesus did. He helped me to wrap up my pain and suffering, my perseverance, my obedience, my hopes, desires, wishes, and nicely place them down in the grave and walk away from my loss in a respectful way.

Lazarus did not come walking out when I rolled the stone. I did not get what I wanted. I experienced death. My own "death." Then God, our Father, resurrected me!

When we face death, the loss of something significant, and respond to it in a respectful way, we can walk away from it. Death doesn't have to own us. It becomes a part of our story. It is not the end of the story.

I believe my "death" was experienced not only for my resurrection but very possibly as a light to yours.

> *"The thief comes only to steal and kill and destroy. I came that they may have life and have it abundantly."* ~JOHN 10:10 (ESV)

Jesus came to do this very thing and His power works in us as we conquer death and continue to share His love.

> *"You intended to harm me, but God intended it for good to accomplish what is now being done, the saving of many lives."* ~GENESIS 50:20

You have pain. I am sure many of you have experienced "death." Our Father did not cause this pain in your life, the thief did. Allow God to walk you through the lies of the enemy to the other side of truth so that you may nicely fold your grave cloths and walk freely into the light.

"Necessary death"

When I was wrestling with the Lord over death, I desperately prayed for wisdom and understanding for the purpose. One evening He answered me so clearly through scripture and a devotion that I laughed out loud in amazement!

> *"What you sow does not come to life unless it dies."*
> ~1 CORINTHIANS 15:36

To further that, these four truths were presented to me in a devotion:[5]

1. Trust God to do it His way.
2. Trust God to answer prayer.
3. Trust God to resurrect.
4. Trust God to fight your battles.

"For you have need of endurance, so that after you have done the will of God, you may receive what is promised." ~HEBREWS 10:36 (ESV)

Caterpillar no longer

Did you know that moth caterpillars spin a chrysalis just like a butterfly? However, they also develop a tough outer casing called a cocoon as they transform. Butterflies on the other hand undergo this transformation right out in the open. Not hidden under a cocoon.[6] Did you also know that moths tend to be out more at night, while butterflies fly by day? I am in amazement at all of God's creation; however, something about the butterfly that flies while the sun is shining down, transforming into something beautiful without hiding the process got me thinking...

I better understand now why a "death" was necessary in my "butterfly moment." The Academy of Natural Sciences of Drexel University[7] displays the Butterfly Life Cycle in four stages:

1. Egg
2. Caterpillar: The Feeding Stage
3. Pupa: The Transition Stage
4. Adult: The Reproductive Stage

It goes on to say that the caterpillar's job was to eat. In our analogy, take that as eating up God's Word and life experiences. The adult's job is to mate and lay eggs. In the cycle noted at the end of each chapter, that means "create." For us, I believe that is creating believers by professing what God is doing in our lives and how He can save. Furthermore, it states "flying comes in handy," because caterpillars can't travel. Yet another important truth to our transformation, professing our faith and traveling far and wide to share it.

A "death" has to happen for that beautiful transformation to begin. Ultimately the caterpillar's existence must end in order for it to transition to its final form.

"Special cells that were present in the larva rapidly grow to become important pieces of the butterfly: legs, wings, and eyes. Those larva cells will also provide energy for the growing adult cells."[8]

Our "caterpillar life" was significant. It became the fuel we needed to develop the hands and feet of Jesus, the wings to travel far and wide to share His truth, and the eyes to see others and the world the way God does. The life we lived as a caterpillar, while significant, has to die in order for us to complete our transformation and allow those experiences and that time to intricately grow our wings and new body.

> *A caterpillar had to die, only to be resurrected by God as something significantly more beautiful—a butterfly.*

A caterpillar had to die, only to be resurrected by God as something significantly more beautiful—a butterfly. When was the last time you missed a butterfly flying by? When was the last time you saw a caterpillar? Often camouflaged, the caterpillar stays hidden, but the butterfly seems to say, "Look at what God did to me when I wrapped up in His protection!" No matter what stage you are in, it is vitally important to the process. God didn't just make butterflies, He made caterpillars, with the plan of transformation at just the right time that would utilize all of the pieces of that caterpillar it had inside.

Transitions are painful. If you have been through childbirth, you know the transition stage is right as the baby moves down the birth canal to come out. Painful, yet it is necessary to "create new."

When we roll stones and the grave turns up empty, God is doing something. He is doing something even bigger than raising someone from the dead. He is providing us an opportunity to "face death" and raise ourselves from the dead to new life. We get a chance to face our worst fears and survive. That is empowering. Jesus did not sit in the tomb staring at the walls, dwelling on His death. He got up, folded up his burial cloths, nicely laid them down, and walked away.

And we can too.

Take one last look at the death you grieve. Acknowledge it. Feel it. Take in the lessons and growth you have received from it. Cry. Yell. Be still. Then, face one more fear: let it go. Walk away from it. Stand outside the tomb, acknowledge what happened, and live a new life beyond the grave, beyond the chrysalis, while glistening white in your fresh, new attire of butterfly wings. Reconnect with those who walked with you as you approached death and let them see you set free of it.

"Those who sow with tears will reap with songs of joy. Those who go out weeping, carrying seed to sow, will return with songs of joy, carrying sheaves with them." ~PSALM 126:5-6

Death leaves a God-sized pain that can only be healed with a miracle that He can perform—resurrection. And while the person, situation, or dream in your life may not resurrect in the way that you would hope, He is fully capable of resurrecting you beyond the grave where your pain lays.

It may not feel like happily ever after, but it isn't time for that yet. That is coming. We need Jesus to return to fully restore things on Earth like they are in Heaven. In the meantime, we need to stick with the flock our Father has led us to and wait with anticipation for those gates to open as we barrel through and start our happily ever after together in full restoration with Him in Heaven.

Until recently, I was unaware that Monarch butterflies migrate south to Mexico. Can you imagine the sight of millions of beautiful butterflies filling the sky on their way to the "light" they are seeking?

I can't wait to see you there, celebrate together, and admire your butterfly wings as we take to the sky as a kaleidoscope of colors flying to the light!

Until that day, remember this: Just as God sent a rainbow to provide a symbol of hope after the flood, we can be rainbows every day to those around us. Reflecting God's light to those we encounter as we live in color and provide hope. His light can fill us and reflect a rainbow through our tears on the best days and even the hardest.

So as you choose your next steps, remember that God restores all that has been lost.

Deuteronomy 30 (MSG), "*³ God, your God, will restore everything you lost; He'll have compassion on you; He'll come back and pick up the pieces from all the places where you were scattered.*"

"*⁸ And you will make a new start, listening obediently to God, keeping all His commandments that I'm commanding you today.*"

"*⁹ God, your God, will outdo Himself in making things go well for you: you'll have babies, get calves, grow crops, and enjoy an all-around good life. Yes, God will start enjoying you again, making things go well for you just as He enjoyed doing it for your ancestors.*"

"*¹⁰ But only if you listen obediently to God, your God, and keep the commandments and regulations written in this Book of Revelation. Nothing halfhearted here; you must return to God, your God, totally, heart and soul, holding nothing back.*"

Will you join me on the path to surrender?

Today, I surrender:
my life.

Lord, show me
the next step
I must take.

Chapter 9
Goals & Discussion

Are you living in restoration?

"Therefore, if anyone is in Christ, he is a new creation. The old has passed away; behold, the new has come." ~2 CORINTHIANS 5:17

Our story has returned to the "Creation" portion of our cycle. Have you been able to allow Jesus into your life to repent of past sins and create a new you?

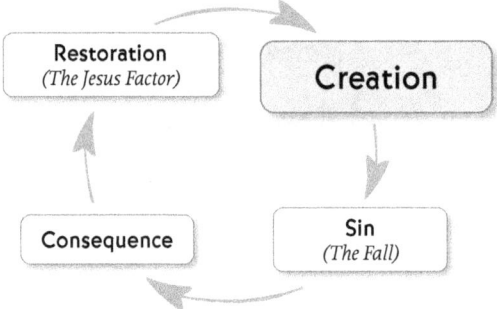

Action Step

Questions to ponder:

1. What stage of surrender do you think you are in and why?

    a. Caterpillar

    b. Chrysalis

    c. Butterfly

2. What elements of your life could evolve or transition so that you can surrender further?

3. What changes in your life have you noticed in your process of surrender?

4. Can you identify a lost sheep in your life that you feel God may be nudging you to connect with so that you can help him/her to rejoin the flock?

    a. What can you do right now to take a step to help that person without taking on the role of "saving," which is God's job!

5. What "death" have you experienced or do you fear experiencing?

    a. How can you fold your grave cloths and walk away?

    b. Can you envision that death as a caterpillar, expectantly, excitedly on the verge of becoming a butterfly?

Epilogue

As I type the last words that were imprinted on my heart to you, it has become important to me to leave you with this.

My surrender, your surrender, OUR surrender...it isn't done. Even if the path seems too daunting or you feel caught up on one step. Just keep going. Walk on, one more step. Surrender is a daily commitment. Even I, writing a book about it, struggle to surrender every part of me every day and have to revisit this concept. We are in this together.

My hope is that no matter where you are, we can meet in a common place that we do need help to let go and let God's will be done.

It takes awareness.

It takes support.

It takes courage.

It takes commitment.

Will you take a step toward surrender today?

Resources

Daily Devotions
Find a source of daily scripture. Here are a few I relied on:
- *Jesus Calling*, Sarah Young
- 365 day desk calendar with scripture
- Wall calendar with scripture
- *Our Daily Bread* (Free devotion online: https://odb.org or print version)

Technology/Apps
Let the Lord infuse your technology. So many free options—here are just a few:
- Bible in a Year (many options)
- Verse of the day (many options for phone apps or email)
- Proverbs 31 daily emails (proverbs31.org)
- Set a reminder on your phone to a specific verse at a difficult time of day for you
- *Heal Body*, Louise Hay app

Books
Books that can help you find your God-given "ness":
- *Purpose Driven Life*, Rick Warren
- *Circle Maker*, Mark Batterson
- *Sacred Parenting*, Gary Thomas
- *Heaven is for Real*, Todd & Sonja Burpo
- *Heaven Changes Everything*, Todd Burpo
- *You Can Heal Your Life*, Louise Hay
- *The Armor of God*, Priscilla Shirer

Songs

Fill your home and vehicle or work place with worship. It dramatically changes the energy of the room and your spirit! Choose a new radio station or search on YouTube and create your own play list. Here are a few to get you started:

- "Great Are You Lord," Casting Crowns
- "My Story," Big Daddy Weave
- "Control," 10th Avenue North
- "Rescue," Lauren Daigle
- "Reckless Love," Cory Asbury
- "Overwhelmed," Big Daddy Weave
- "So Will I," Tori Kelly
- "Come Alive Dry Bones," Lauren Daigle
- "Raise a Hallelujah," Jonathan and Melissa Helser
- "Spirit Lead Me," Michael Ketterer and Influence Music
- "Changed," Jordan Feliz
- "Available," Elevation Worship
- "I Surrender," Hillsong Worship
- "Love Never Fails," Brandon Heath
- "I've Been Redeemed," Big Daddy Weave
- "You Say," Lauren Daigle

Movies/Television

Choose programming that will uplift and encourage you. So many options, but here are a couple that have been influential to our home:

- *Bible: The Epic Miniseries* 4-Disc DVD set (Brought the Bible to life for me and got me actually reading it!)
- *Passion of the Christ*, Mel Gibson (2004)

- *War Room*, Alex Kendrick (2015)
- *The Mingling of Souls: God's Design for Love, Marriage, Sex, and Redemption*, Matt Chandler (Books and Videos online)
- *Right Now Media* (Netflix meets the Bible! Your local library or church may be able to get you connected.)

Personal inventory

Utilize other tools to explore who you are and what unique traits you have to offer the world. Have fun exploring yourself. Celebrate YOU!

- Character strengths
  https://www.viacharacter.org/character-strengths
- Love Languages
  https://www.5lovelanguages.com/
- Growth Mindset
  https://www.growthmindsetinstitute.org/
- True Colors
  https://truecolorsintl.com/the-four-color-personalities/
  (This one has a cost, but contact your local extension office to see if a free program is offered or look for other options online.)

Local Community Engagement

Find resources near you to get connected with your flock.

- Celebrate Recovery (https://www.celebraterecovery.com/)
- Campus ministries—if you are in college, seek out the campus ministries your university has to offer!
- Pray for God to lead you to:
  - The best church fit for you
  - Study or support groups for you
  - A Godly leader or Christian counselor to assist you as you take steps toward surrender.

References

Part 1: Caterpillar

Introduction
Bible References:
- Ecclesiastes 3:1-8
- Matthew 7:7
- 2 Chronicles 20:15

1. Spread Truth. *The Story Maker*. Available at TheStoryMaker.com
2. Languages, *Oxford Concise Oxford American Dictionary*. Oxford University Press, 2006

Chapter 1: I See You
Bible References:
- Jeremiah 1:5
- Zephaniah 3:17
- James 4:8
- Deuteronomy 31:8
- John 3:16
- Galatians 5:22-23
- Matthew 5:12
- Psalm 139:5
- Psalm 23:4
- 1 Peter 5:8
- Ephesians 1:23

1. *You, Me, and Dupree* DVD, 2006
2. Warren, Rick. *What on Earth Am I Here For? Purpose Driven Life*. Zondervan, 2002

3. Unknown, Author. Available at: http://www.projecthappiness.org
4. Unknown, Author. Association for Psychological Science—APS. Available at: http://www.psychologicalscience.org

Chapter 2: "I Got This!"

Bible References:
- Philippians 4:6-7
- Luke 15:6-7
- Ephesians 5:21
- Matthew 5:21-23
- Galatians 5:19-21
- James 4:17
- Romans 3:23
- 2 Thessalonians 3:3

Chapter 3: To My Knees

Bible References:
- John 1:9
- Ephesians 4:14
- Jeremiah 29:11
- Hebrews 5:12-14
- 1 Peter 5:8
- 1 Corinthians 10:13

1. *Passion of the Christ*, Mel Gibson DVD, 2004
2. Warren, Rick. *What on Earth Am I Here For? Purpose Driven Life.* Zondervan, 2002

Part 2: Chrysalis

Chapter 4: Finding Fellowship

Bible References:

- 1 Thessalonians 5:11

Chapter 5: Rylie, "And God breathed new life into me"

Bible References:

- Isaiah 43:19
- Proverbs 18:4

1. Unknown, Author. Untitled Page. Available at: http://www.celebraterecovery.com

2. Ministries, Discovery House Publishers, Our Daily Bread. *Our Daily Bread*. Discovery House Pub

3. Burpo, Todd Burpo, Sonja. *Heaven Changes Everything*. Thomas Nelson, 2012

Chapter 6: Pressure is Mounting

Bible References:

- Psalm 38:6
- 1 Corinthians 6:19

1. Unknown, Author. Untitled Page. Available at: http://www.Courses.lumenlearning.com

2. Rowland, Amy Z. *Traditional Reiki for Our Times*. Inner Traditions / Bear & Co, 1998

3. Davidson, Libby Barnett, Maggie Chambers, Susan. *Reiki Energy Medicine*. Inner Traditions / Bear & Co, 1996

4. Hay, Louise. *You Can Heal Your Life*, Gift Edition. Hay House, Inc, 1999

5. Unknown, Author. Home—Bruce H. Lipton, PhD. Available at: http://www.brucelipton.com

6. *Evan Almighty*, Tom Shadyac (2007)

Chapter 7: The Mud and the Mire
Bible References:
- Psalm 41:2
- 1 Corinthians 7:12-14
- 1 Samuel 1:27-28

1. Unknown, Author. Oxford Languages and Google—English | Oxford Languages. Available at: https://languages.oup.com/google-dictionary-en/

Chapter 8: Sam, "And God taught me to let it go"
Bible References:
- Isaiah 43:18-19
- John 3:16
- Ephesians 6
- Proverbs 25:1

1. Hay, Louise. *You Can Heal Your Life*, Gift Edition. Hay House, Inc, 1999

Part 3: Butterfly

Chapter 9: Becoming a Butterfly

Bible References:
- Psalm 40:1-4
- Galatians 5:22-23
- Deuteronomy 20:4
- Jeremiah 29:11-12
- Psalm 46:5
- Ephesians 6:14
- Joshua 24:8
- Acts 22:16
- Chronicles 20:17
- John 11:39
- Matthew 27:46
- John 20:6-7
- John 10:10
- Genesis 50:20
- 1 Corinthians 15:36
- Hebrews 10:36
- Psalm 126:5-6
- Deuteronomy 30

1. Batterson, Mark Batterson, Parker. *The Grave Robber*. Baker Books, 2015
2. *Avengers: End Game,* Anthony & Joe Russo, 2019

3. Ministries, Discovery House Publishers, Our Daily Bread. Cetas, Anne. A Place of Belonging. *Our Daily Bread.* Discovery House Pub, 2019

4. Wilke, Richard Byrd and Kitchens, Julia. *Disciple: Under the Tree of Life Study Manual.* 2001.

5. Gumbel, Nicky and Pippa. BIOY app daily devotional.

6. Unknown, Author. Home—Science NetLinks. Available at: http://www.sciencenetlinks.com

7. Unknown, Author. The Academy of Natural Sciences of Drexel University. Available at: http://www.ansp.org

8. Ibid.

A Special Thank You

Thank you sincerely to all who helped me bring this God-breathed vision to life!

Mom and Dad, thank you for taking this journey of healing with me and joining with me to share this story. It takes courage to allow God to shine through our broken places and I am grateful you, in a supportive way, allowed me to do so. I trust He will save many lives with our truth.

Thank you to Ryan for allowing me to share personal stories during painful times we experienced together. Your courage to do this I trust will help many others do the same.

Thank you to all of my friends and family who took time and energy to read and provide me feedback to make this a work that is valuable to the reader and glorifying to God.

Thank you to my children, Rylie and Sam, for listening to my stories and desiring to learn more and grow in your relationship with God. Thank you for being my audience as I prepared this work for the readers. Your very existence brought this to life! I love you.

Julie Anne Fehrenbacher took her love of science and helping others to launch a career as a Registered Dietitian. This path led her to become a Foodservice Director and Wellness Coordinator at a Public School District where she realized her passion to help those in need and children. She gained an appreciation for research, data collection, and authorship in this role as she worked with graduate students on thesis research and prepared presentations to her staff and community about nutrition and wellness. After having her own two boys, she surrendered herself to the Lord and asked that He use her skills to build the next chapter of her life. He developed her ability to teach and disciple students as a science teacher in Christian secondary education. The Lord then led her to take all of these skills home to homeschool her own children and complete this work. She hopes to empower all readers with the belief that they can experience abundant life and freedom through surrender and take their next step.

Julie lives with her two sons, two guinea pigs, two hamsters, snail, and dog. They love playing games and spending time outdoors.

www.ingramcontent.com/pod-product-compliance
Lightning Source LLC
Chambersburg PA
CBHW051438290426
44109CB00016B/1606